For the Class of 1985

For the Class of 1985

FOR THE CLASS OF 1985

First edition. February 01, 2025.

Second edition. June 06, 2025.

Copyright © 2025 James E. Keller.

ISBN: 979-8-9924637-3-6

Library of Congress Control Number: 2025902946

Written by James E. Keller.

Artwork Copyright © 2025 James E. Keller and Elaine C. Keller

For the Class of 1985

Table of Contents

You can teach the Golden Rule without teaching children about transvestites. If that poses a horrible logistical problem then move to Europe.

Comments for the Second Edition

This second edition was triggered by a little discussion, which happened gradually after a few people realized that I can take criticism. They commented that the first edition needed more focus.

I said, "I just wanted to write a few stories to my high school class."

One said, "Yeah, but even they will want a better point."

Another said, "Think about it."

Then the first one added, "People don't read books without controversy or romance. Controversy is gossip. Sex is attractive. People love that." Then she added, "They also like motivational diet books."

So…

Here we are.

I guess I could take off some of my clothes as I type this next part. Although, on second thought, I'll keep my clothes on…for now.

But the next 10 pages aim to be controversial…and *sexy*.

Monkeys, Bread & Vaccines

When I was little, in the summer of 1972 or '73, my father took me on a train trip from Los Angeles to San Diego. We went to the zoo. A lot of other boys and their fathers were on the same trip. I thought it was odd and unfair that there were no father-daughter pairs but I was too little to think critically. In a short time though, I became much less concerned about girls. They would have probably felt better not being there. Every inch of the zoo was covered with asphalt and concrete. It was so hot, I wondered why the ground didn't melt.

The only other memorable thing about the whole trip was watching an angry monkey climb an artificial hill while spastically screeching at all the other sweltering monkeys that were sitting around up there. One wondered how that animal could have so much energy on such a miserable day. After reaching the pinnacle, and while trying to look prominent, the noisy one squatted to sit, then instantly shot up like a compressed spring.

One of the fathers near me calmly said, "I think it just burned its butt." All of us little boys giggled. As if in response, the beast glared up at us (we were standing on an overlook) and howled & showed its teeth.

And as it became more frustrated, we giggled more...then laughed...

...which made it angrier and angrier.

From its hilltop, it ignored us briefly, looked around as if uninterested; it stretched its legs to stand tall and upright, looked over its vast, dusty enclosure, forgot about the heat and tried to sit again...which triggered the repeated spring, screech, spastic rage, making us giggle then laugh...And the animal became more and more aggravated with us.

I assumed it was a male, but if we could go back and ask it which pronouns it preferred, I guess it would use sign language to say, "He/Him/His". But like goth/transvestite/hypersexuals, the monkey is still an "it" in my book.

How was that?
> *Was that controversial?*
>> *No?*
>>> *Give me another chance...*

6

If you ask parents whether they think a particular playground is safe, you will get four types of answers: (1) a flippant one, (2) a nuanced one, (3) a stupid one and (4) one from the guy who wasn't listening. Everyone knows that safety is not a number on an elevator button. Safety is an assessment. And it is tailored to each situation for each person.

The same is probably true for airplane safety. When I get on a plane, I am always nervous. If something goes wrong, I figure it will be catastrophic. Either the plane flies well or I will not be able to talk about the trip.

Statistics don't help. An AI algorithm can spit out bullshit to make me feel like someone knows something, but my confidence doesn't change.

Engineers will tell you that air flight, like playing on a playground, has shades of danger. It's possible, they will say, that 10,000 things can go wrong without affecting the flight. However, given my preeminent lack of knowledge, and in spite of these reassurances, I fly on faith alone.

Vaccine safety is like flying. We have varying degrees of acceptance of this. We are usually resigned and accept our fate; some of us are graceful about this; most of us grudgingly go along.

For our children, vaccine safety falls somewhere between airplane safety and playground safety. In some ways, getting our child vaccinated is like putting a child onto a plane and walking away. Some people might feel relieved or even euphoric watching their child leave for a short trip or watch them get a shot that is supposed to protect them. Others might need sedation and counseling. I fall nearer this latter side but usually settle for ibuprofen and maybe a nap.

Being over-protective is a form of abuse. Some parents are too controlling. Some nag. Some hover. Or are manipulative. And lecture too much. However, children who are respectful towards others deserve complete liberty to manage themselves. When a child has a moral compass, then it's time to let the child use it. Proper thinking requires practice. Practice is tiring. Part of our job, therefore, is to balance worry and respect for our children, which means giving them time and space to make decisions. And, that means, letting them travel without us, sometimes. It also means trying not to fill their heads with too much noise.

Part of our collective problem in the United States is that we adults are regularly free to make only two types of decisions: (1) we are free to make a perfectly legal, robotic stop at the next STOP sign we see and (2) we are free to make a doctor's appointment to get another shot. When any community has so little freedom and so little opportunity to exercise simple thoughts to make reasonable decisions, then when choices become available to us, we are resentful no matter how simple and clear the topic is.

For example, some people say that the Republicans are anti-science for taking advantage of the anti-vaccine movement. Yet, the Republicans are not foisting laws to forbid vaccine sales. If a thousand politicians say they are against vaccines, 80 million families and their family doctors are not going to stop exercising good judgement. We don't need a federal policy for everything.

I'm pretty annoyed that over the past 40 years, every time a measles outbreak has occurred, cameras and microphones have been jammed into the face of a public health advocate who wrings his hands, soils his pants and says that only 90% of Americans are vaccinated, and that the end of times is upon us...

Woe is us. A world of horror and indecency is descending. Please subscribe to my channel. And don't forget to smash LIKE to save us.

It's these constant instructions that kill me. *"Don't forget"*, *"Subscribe today"*, *"Get your vaccine today"* or *"Don't get your vaccine. It causes brain damage."* All these interest groups seem to take turns shouting into the crack between my legs hoping to make me change my mind about something. They never shut up.

Well. Let's recap: over the past 40 years, everything causes brain damage. Too much sun, too little sun, too much caffeine, not enough alcohol, poor air quality, too many peanuts among the mixed nuts, not enough raisins in raisin bread...Part of the solution to this insanity is to bake your own damned raisin bread. It works well. It's easy.

When my son was three or four, at an airport waiting to fly to Japan, he said the TVs had a lot of noisy faces. The "noisy faces" term was his contribution to my vocabulary: TV news is nothing more than monkeys fighting on a hot, fake hilltop…apparently trying to shout into my crack.

The world is a dirty place. You want your family to live in a safe community surrounded by people like Adam's son, Abel. But you know his other son, Cain, is never far away. And Cain will always try to smear filth on your child…then he will laugh about it. And he will be proud about causing harm. Then he or his lawyer will blame you for giving your child too much liberty and respect.

Avoiding vaccines raises an important point about balancing responsibility against bleeding-heart liberals who want to push you away from wisdom, away from decent community life. Everything is a spinning conspiracy with noisy TV faces. The Cains are like a collective Shakespearean narrator who build trust, then speak a short key sentence to trigger suspicion. They introduce doubt to guide otherwise ideal & good people into a quagmire of paranoia.

Concern is worry without hysteria. *Courage* is bravery woven with awareness. Good parenting needs *concern* and *courage* but most of the time our social world pushes us towards drama – into a self-inflicted, confused downward spiral.

I told my children that the anti-vaccine noise from politicians is primitive capitalism, Caveman Capitalism. When the first caveman invented bread, and gained fame and social status, Caveman B (one of the early Cains) got upset. He said, "Unga bunga banga…", which means, "Don't eat that bread. It's poisonous. It will give you and your children brain damage. It'll disrupt the hunt. Crops will not grow. It will make bugs bite harder, you will get worms, and then you will itch."

Later, after Caveman B learned to make bread, he said, "Binga bunga boh," which means, "Oh…I fixed it. You can eat this bread. It's safe."

After anti-vax politicians dig their fingers into the current action, and force the vaccine industry to give them a financial cut, I guess they will say, "Oh…we fixed everything. It's ok to get vaccines. Ours are safe."

I was told this was still not controversial enough.

Let's try again.

9

For the Class of 1985

The Sinner

If you make a loser
feel like a winner…

     you will gain a friend who,
      with an optimistic glimmer,
       will gladly kill
        to suit your will,
         like a proud, but antsy sinner.
          With or without much skill,
           and without a growing, costly bill…
            he'll always welcome you to his home,
            for a warm & fancy dinner…

              …maybe, at times,
               with fava beans
                and a well-cooked liver.

Sorry. I don't know where this came from. It had no sex, and only made a passing reference to inspirational weight-loss.

I think the next few pages are much better…

Transvestites and other Hypersexuals are Degenerates

To be controversial, I could write about transvestites. But I don't know much about Goths or other hypersexuals. I don't watch news programs. Sometimes I read headlines, though, which means I might be an expert by a small margin.   So, here we go then: Transvestites.

If I had to teach children that either (A) the Earth is flat or (B) that transvestitism is something they should consider as part of their progression through early pre-pubescence, I would teach them that the Earth is flat. Transvestitism is anti-science. Well, both concepts are anti-science. But the shape of the world has less permanence on a child's mind than the impact of lying to them about their bodies, and manipulating their minds to create circumstances where they never trust their surroundings. It prevents them from growing in age-appropriate ways. Every time a transvestite inhales he is lying to himself. Every time the transvestite exhales, he is lying to the world. Therefore, all such anti-science agendas should go back to hell.

I am not saying that all Trans people are imaginary. I believe without hesitation that God created difficulties including sexual identity and even homosexuality. However, not only should both issues be excluded from schools (especially for young children), but neither of these qualities pose unique difficulties in childhood compared to anything or anybody else. If we were to go back to 1972 and force schools to implement a "Tall, Skinny, Heterosexual White boy Appreciation Month," I would not feel good about it. When I started kindergarten, I wanted to play with other children – boys and girls. Skin color and other adult obsessions had nothing to do with it. I didn't want special attention from whacked out strangers. I certainly did not want a bunch of men in women's clothing walking into the school to "appreciate" me.

As a child, I was not strong enough to play rough with most boys and I wasn't fast enough to chase and catch girls, nor was I quick-witted. I was probably bossy at times but I was never a fast talker. Also, back then, the playground was divided between a girls' side and a boys' side. The teachers did not enforce this but the girls did. Their side was painted and decorated nicely and was very colorful. On the boys' side, we had a three-foot diameter sewer pipe to crawl through or climb on. I didn't think that was fair. Sometimes, I wanted to swing and laugh with the girls.

As much as I wanted to be friendly with as many children as possible, I was physically and socially unable to achieve that desire. I had to accommodate my circumstances. My poor, suffering emotional isolation in childhood does not mean we must revamp American public schools to teach children to fondle themselves or to decide whether they need surgical correction. My way was unpleasant. The other way is sick.

Back in kindergarten, I made friends with a small number of boys and girls. We were at about the same level. This is life. We didn't need transvestite men showing up to put their agenda into the classroom. As a child, I desired to be like everyone, but I wasn't. Saying that a Trans child is somehow unique on this front is a lie because nobody is like everyone. Average people do not exist. We are all excluded somehow.

I suspect that all social problems in childhood are on par with Trans children. When I was five or six years old, a man told me and another boy that we should try holding hands and kissing. He said if we did, we would never need to have girlfriends. "He's your boyfriend, right?" he asked.

I said, "We're friends but we're not boyfriends."

He said, "But you're both boys, so that makes you boyfriends." He explained that if we kissed and touched each other, we would realize how good it is. He wanted us to help each other pee, too.

The transvestite agenda today follows the same degenerate path as that from the 1970s. Today the perverts have refined their messages and they have much more power and funding. Their motive is unchanged, though, and remains just as immoral as it was all those years ago.

The statistics point to a genetic identity crises affecting 0.03% of school-aged children. If we exaggerate this and add other psychological (non-genetic, YouTube, TikToc) influencing, we can increase this to 0.1%. Assuming I am way way wrong, let's exaggerate it further to 0.5%. The other 99.5% of children should not have to see or listen to men wearing women's clothing while manipulating everyone in a classroom.

We are all adaptable. We are accommodating. These are the two levers the Cains pull to bring equality and harmony. It's nonsense.

We want our children to live free of these Cains. But since the Cains will never leave us alone, our children must be able to recognize the evil ones. Cain hides his cruelty under layers of fake kindness. He is like the Coachman from Pinocchio. He will help you for an immoral price. And he will not be satisfied until he sinks his claws into a child's soft underbelly and asks, "Are you sure you want to be a real boy?" He repeats this incessantly while looking for other boys, adding them to his bin, ignoring any emotional pain and tying them down with a cold, heavy chain as they all travel to the playful Land of Cokaigne…where Pinocchio eventually turns into a jackass.

It has many names: raping, grooming, manipulating, lying. *If you make a loser feel like a winner, the loser loses for a very long time.* Manipulators, like rich kids from Hollywood and their lawyers, believe that a loser is at rock bottom. They are predators and vultures. Weak and vulnerable children become fair game. Remember Shirley Temple's child porn scenes from the 1930s? To these men, stage moms and strippers are identical; they are partially burned cigarettes still smoldering, still overly fragrant with acrid effervescence. To the vultures, this dysfunction is ingrained in many women. And if a vulture can wave a $100 bill to get a woman to do what he wants, that is attractive. It is something the Coachman would do; aiming for little boys instead.

I cannot help but see a nauseating connection between the transvestite agenda today and the Goths of the 1980s. Over these decades, the Goths or their rich handlers have honed their message. Back in the day, they targeted young adults who were stuck living pay-check to pay-check.

In the early 1990s, I met a young woman who was a little older than me. She was pretty. She was a former stripper but when I met her, we were both living a hundred miles up the California coast outside of Los Angeles. She had seen me eating lunch in my car. So, she walked up and asked me to join her. We began regularly sitting together eating next to that parking lot. One time, in the midst of a brief chat, she casually said, "You'd never believe how often men offered to pay for plastic surgery."

She looked perfectly proportional to me. Nothing seemed unusual until she pointed out that the freckles on her cheeks were small holes that someone had drilled so she could slide in fake whiskers to make her look like a cat or a bunny or some other furry animal. Otherwise, during her day-job doing secretarial work, she looked like a simple, attractive young woman. She said she had gone through a Goth-phase but after moving out of LA, she tried to settle down to avoid constant anxiety.

Nowadays, instead of targeting desperate strippers and drug addicky teenagers, the Goth degenerates (and their handlers) target preschoolers. Wealthy handlers are the bigger problem. These are the ones who quietly offer to pay for plastic surgery; they encourage Goths and transvestites to cut their bodies; or get them to have those fake horns surgically implanted; get another tattoo, and rise up to sex organ piercings…the handlers pay whatever is needed to get people to debase themselves. But like all sex obsessions, the handlers became bored and apparently set their sights on less accessible and more exciting prey. In the early 2000s, they began going after children electronically. We heard about these private idahos, we got more sophisticated Shirley Temple videos, and we had to hear about more and more Wacko Jacko sleep-overs. These degenerate things didn't go away. They never stopped. They were simply refined using email and online chats.

If a man says, "Hey, little boy, why don't you touch yourself down there, and if you don't like it, if you think it feels strange…or you don't like the way it looks, smells or…tastes, then ask your mommy to take you to the doctor to have it fixed," it's evil. This is grooming. It is abuse. However, if the man wears women's clothes and says the same things, then it's DEI. It's A-ok. Open the school doors, bring him into the PTA meetings, give'em a microphone and let him debase your child. Debasing is the goal.

I want to be clear that there is a difference between people who are naturally born as homosexual/transexual; a second group who adapt to one or the other of these "ways of life" to deal with their circumstances; and a third group who use these people to advance their sexual degenerate agenda(s). Good people can adapt to all sorts of horrible and unnatural things. This adaptability is natural. In fact, the Trans and Homo manipulators seem to *always* ignore this when defending their degenerate desires. They never acknowledged that people, children in particular, can be misled.

We, as a nation have a mixed record on how we deal with these various circumstances. Throughout American history, different parts of our country have had graded sympathies towards accepting people from troubled backgrounds. Hypersexuals, on the other hand, are more interested in manipulation, not fairness or acceptance.

In our modern times, "natural" homosexuals have been forced to associate with hypersexual degenerates even though these groups have nothing in common. The sexual labels simply group people according to where their mouths go instead of considering what their minds think. The degenerates use these unnatural associations to foist themselves onto children. They claim they are just misunderstood like all the other LGBTWD4oLx2, and they aim to tie the "naturals" to the degenerates with an unbreakable emotional chain. It is similar to going into a bar and encouraging a stripper to get pierced and plasticized... then give her a little too much alcohol...then marijuana, then coke, to slowly debase her and get her to feel like this is her fault, her own doing.

To *debase* is to *destroy* any sense of a normal life. Debasing is mockery from the powerful who look down on the poor. They celebrate each time they de-flower someone. The problem with these scum is that they get bored easily. They need to expand their horizons, which leads them to aim for things that are normally out of reach like, for example, potty rights for transvestite kindergarteners.

...

Shamefully, I cannot remember the name of the pretty young woman. I think her real name was Laurie but at different times she said her name was Amber or Amy, then later added another name which was like "Saphire" or one of those new-age, hippie names that evoke a color and a spirit. But I forget. It was a nice name...whatever it was.

She had a horrible background, though;

Poetically fractured:

like this...

For the Class of 1985

The Stoned Debasers

After Rock-n-Roll
  came Punk-n-Droll.
    When Goths arrived without music or soul
      they blanketed Los Angeles
        like an army of degenerates
          with spirit stones, pink salts and magical "vita-minalists";
            And, tho', they struggled and floited like moths under
          up-turned glasses & bowls;
            they sang inspirational songs
            about sado-masochists,
              while they played with their tired asses & holes.

Vampires moved quickly down Ventura Boulevard,
  moving west towards a Malibu flame...
    Using daddy's cash and name...
      and his gold-plated credit card;
        Soon, eyes burned from too much cocaine,
          which is not hard to do when you are lost & insane.
        Faces were marred
          with blood & snot;
          While tattoos & piercings became
            common & tame, for this sorry lot.
              Overall, Goths spent too much time
                sucking weed, injecting heroin,
                  PCP and all kinds of other exciting
                what-not.

And oh they complain...
  The Goths say,
    everyone else is a pain
      by using English in inappropriate
      sexist, and impolite ways.
        Outsiders are always to blame,
          as the Goths confidently proclaim
            that "s/he" can shit in many inspiring ways
            which is a tiny part of their playful aim
              as they play Hollywood's shadowy, dirty
              black backyard sex game.

For the Class of 1985

The Stoned Debasers
(2 of 3)

The Stripper worked, like in the Valley of shadows and bright lights.
She was soon, like, offered silicone butt cheeks and bolstered hips
with, like, complimentary fattened-up lips,
and because she was so… *witty*,
she, like, also got (among other delights)
this strange 50% deal for a two-for-one artificial…*titty*,
and, like, she got a nose job and a clit slit-n-pealing,
which was, like, somewhat appealing.
And, like, she was totally willing
to get like holes drilled
into her cheeks, like,
as highlights…
because like she identified as
a cute, shy, little… *kitty*.
With the new holes
she could like slide
fake whiskers inside
without losing
pride or
getting too
much shit
or *pitty*.

Soon the thin little kitten,
wearing clothes that were too sheer and
uncomfortable to sit in
became entirely smitten;
And her new role, she easily embraced;
after being completely debased.
Then she happily free-based
a little more black-tar heroin.

For the Class of 1985

The Stoned Debasers
(3 of 3)

A rich kid from Malibu, The Palisades, or West Hills,
    paid for everything, leaving her with no outstanding bills,
      and promising her a bright star,
         he even got her a new, pink-n-white big big car.
        This helped to calm her anxiety and ills,
           yet, he still had to give her a few daily pills,
              which he was happy to supply because these thrills
            enhanced his social skills
            and showcased his life
              up in the wealthy foothills.
                As his sexual fantasy grew…
                    he let the smugness build and build
                    until it was time to make her
                      chew whatever he chose to spew.

Years later, after he had matured and grew,
    and grew harder still,
      with each new girl left behind,
        he surrounded himself with media men
        who were cooperatively aligned,
          which helped him to write immoral charters
            to secretly fund his Gothic partners…
          to focus their blurry sights,
            on Toilet Rights
              for preschool Transvestites,
                and other misguided kindergartners!!

    … proving their political wit & skills…
    from the wealthiest corners of, perhaps,
      Beverely Hills.

Introduction

"Some of the best men I ever worked with in a swindle would resort to trickery at times."

The Ethics of Pig, by O. Henry (1904)

This is not a political book. The nearest I come to writing "Democrats" is when I call them "Demon-craps", "Demoncrapic" or something similar. I never mention Republicans. Well, only a few times. In the 1990s, one of my Army bosses said, "When you point a finger at someone, you have three pointing at yourself." This is an appropriate frame of mind because these days, at my age, my memory is so diminished that I do not remember why I have so many opinions. This book is not supposed to be rude, though. It is actually very thoughtful and considerate. I never use profanity except on rare occasions, and only when necessary (Mark Twain).

Last year, as I realized our 40th reunion was approaching, I was quietly optimistic and began to wonder when and where it would happen. In a short time, however, and after a little thought, I decided I would not fly to California to meet you. I did not attend the 30th or 20th anniversaries, or the 25th or 15th if you had those. I attended the 10th right before I left for the East Coast but I did not meet all of the people I had hoped to, and I have not been in contact with anyone among you, more or less since 1995 as the most recent, and since 1985, in general. So, after being apart for such a long time, I figured that it was inappropriate to attend a high school reunion obligating you to remember me instead of me making an effort to find you ahead of time.

In spite of this self-exile, around Thanksgiving 2024 I began to reminisce, and realized that some of you are dear to my heart. Somewhere in my mind, I have had this decades old beacon reaching out to many of my past friends. The following letter, therefore, is for you, the entire *Class of 1985*, hoping it finds my former classmates in good health and in high spirits, especially as we approach our 60-year birthdays.

At first, I thought 500 or 1000 words would be enough to give you a little update and offer to speak or write to anyone interested. Soon, however, the letter grew to 8,000 words; eventually, peaking at around 44,000. I am so sorry. It should be shorter. Some of the chapters have nice, humorous ramblings, recollections and some brief summaries of events that link our lives to some moments in US history. However, later chapters have sections with offensive humor & relentless criticism of transvestites and quite a lot of criticism of "American" feminism. These were supposed to be examples that you could replace with any social group you disagree with. Every social protest follows the same pattern: it's like commercials for a new breakfast cereal. It never changes much. The feminism criticisms are tame but the transvestite parts took on a bigger role than I had planned.

The point is not to vilify you if you belong to one or both groups. If you get up every morning and try to be a good, fair person, then fine. Be a feminist. Be a transvestite. I don't have the energy to smack people around without knowing their circumstances. Also, there is a distinction between an individual and the political agenda of their chosen group(s). It's easy to put politics aside and take you one at a time. That's decent. That's my goal.

Unintentionally, though, in the second half of the book, some of the narrative became a *Don Quixote*-esque "conservative" quest to fix the world. This is rude and inconsiderate of your time. It is thoughtless towards your hard-earned wisdom built up over your life experiences.

So, if you are kind enough to continue reading my essays, use your best judgement and, if you become offended, skip forward to the next section and refer back to the paragraph above. I aim to be considerate and fair.

With all sincerity, and putting politics aside, my opinions are not important. They are only a sideshow. At face value, I would like to say I am thinking about you in the kindest ways possible. If you are struggling with grief, other hardships, or simply dealing with the creakings of age & high mileage, you have my best wishes, and I'm sure you have the deepest hopes from all the other members of our high school class. I wish you as much comfort as the circumstances allow. If your life has been good up to this point, then count your blessings. Your timer is delayed. That's all. But, regardless of how much or how little grace you have had up to this point, I wish you each good health and much happiness going forward.

This book is a genuine effort to be direct, fair with some humor and a little irony among disjointed chapters to broadly describe how the past 40 years have shaped me. At any rate, if you are not prepared for social commentary then please don't read further. This introduction serves my overall purpose. If you choose to read further, you might try reading the remaining chapters in reverse order. Going from back-to-front might reduce any controversy. Chapter 1 has a little sexuality in it in case you're interested. But I couldn't fit in anything about inspirational dieting.

Sincerely,

The Author.

Chapter 1

Empathy

"I love this country...I love the freedoms we used to have."

George Carlin

In 1985, we graduated from Western High School. We were about 150 young men and 150 young women. Wait? Did that offend you? It did. Oh…it didn't. Sorry. I thought there'd be at least a few sons-of-bitches reading this who would wonder how many transvestites we had. Part of my mind is too suspicious, I guess. You might be the same way, especially if your diet, hormone levels and your noisy AI-tailored commercials overlap with my Google regimen. Anyway, the other parts of my mind are comfortable saying that we didn't have transvestites. But this raises two important points:

!   and   .

Maybe not. Yeah, not really.

Every time a transvestite talks on TV, I imagine Black people in the audience think, *"Please don't call yourself a minority, please don't call yourself a …"* over and over. The expression, "lipstick on a pig" seems to be an apathetic allegory against painful narcotic-like addiction to invented sexual problems and contrived social strain.

Fall and winter should be relaxing, quiet times of the year. However, as 2024 ends, I am tempted to say that bad behavior spewing forth across this country has clogged my mind to the point that I still have difficulty (1) forming simple, uninterrupted, thoughts and (2) writing simple, direct sentences without lawyers, priests, aldermen and other wisemen and wisewomen helping me figure out what type of *freedom of speech* I have and whether it is reasonable to exercise whatever vestiges of it remain.

On the other hand, maybe our country is paradise, and I have slept through its transformation. But I doubt I missed such a change. Acid rain stopped about 30 years ago. That's nice. Yet, if God were to proclaim that the United States should complete the transition and become the New Garden of Eden, people would probably be upset. The stock market would go down, and the *Garden* would need substantial trimming. Porno pimps and their "actresses" who make incest films would have to leave the country. Smash-the-bell, Go-to-Hell. But, as far as I can tell, if paradise is here, it is not doing well.

I never heard Paris Hilton's voice. Or a Kardashian's. I know there are more than one of these but "Kim" is the only name I know. Are they all whores? Or did a few try child-pimping? I never saw the Game of Thrones series; or modern zombie movies; I know there was a famous dragon cartoon in the last 10 or 15 years but I don't care. Anyway, neither of my children have seen it unless it was shown at school during a snow day. Disney is apparently regurgitating its guts and consuming the puke but we haven't seen *Frozen* or any of the others. Not for politics, though.

I know that Brucey Jenner is no longer a man. But even when he was, my freak-dar regularly blasted in the cereal aisle in the 1970s when we passed his picture on all those orange boxes. He was too nauseating to look at even out of drag. I have heard Mr. Obama speak a few times; Mr. Trump, a few times fewer. I have heard them so rarely, that when I watch the rare video clip, my inner narrator challenges the correctness of their voices: Mr. Obama's real voice is a little deeper than it should be, and Mr. Trump's is way too high. I feel AI bots must be changing the audio to make me go nuts. It doesn't matter what the men say because their pitch and tone are distracting. In 2025, I finally heard Lyin' Ted Cruz for the first time. It was a video clip from 2016. He sounded like a girly boy.

Anyhow, I aimed to begin this letter by reminding you of our times together in the 1980s but instead, I had to break away to figure whether it was legal or morally & socially acceptable to list the approximate number of boys and girls in our school. Maybe, I should try a gluten-free, vegan biscuit before writing more.

... ...

The rest of this letter is sincere. We are too old to deal with jerky humor about trans-this, trans-that and trans-fat. So, to begin in earnest now, let me remind you that even though we all graduated together, few of you ever knew the real me. I hesitate about what to say about this.

I recently told my children that I have this unreasonable trust for people who I knew in high school, and I imagine that I can rely on those well-aged old people more than almost anyone else. Thinking back, though, it's completely irrational to trust you. And, the absurdity goes further because I didn't have friendships back then. I never shared secrets, never confided feelings or listened to any of yours.

Perhaps my parents were so busy fighting with, giving back-handed compliments to, or practicing other passive-aggressive nonsense on your parents that I kept my distance. With so much gossip and acrimony, my priorities were to keep breathing, avoid trouble and fade away.

Then in late 2024, I remembered you, the Class of 1985. And, I decided to share some of my most private thoughts in hopes of receiving your blessings and hearing your opinions. Don't worry though. My only homosexual experience happened in the 1990s when I was working for the Army; I accidentally mentioned to a group of sergeants that I owned scented candles and potpourri. That's it. And, it happened at a bar. I was a little drunk. They were a little drunk…And, anyway, I didn't buy the stuff. An ex-girlfriend left those things behind. I do not remember why I raised the topic but wisdom stands upon our life experiences, and although our mistakes shape us, I can't help but feel I was terribly misunderstood. They didn't force me to do anything that I wasn't prepared to do. And I greatly appreciate that one of the sergeants was the sober designated driver. As the only clear-headed one around, he must have protected my naïve ass. And, we all got home safely. But, overall, and looking back: Who knew candles and fragrance were so gay. I simply thought they smelled nice...I mean the candles, not the sergeants. Anyhu...were you freaked out by Brucey Jenner, too?

Before going further, let me clearly state that I strongly identify as a man. This chapter could have been called, "Call Me Mister". So let me refresh your memories about who I was in the 1970s and 80s. Then we will cover my mid-life transition and my shimmering rebirth a few years ago.

The old me

I was James Keller. However, many of you might remember me by my middle name, "Eric". One reason you knew me as "Eric" is because that is how I introduced myself. Another reason is that whenever teachers would call roll asking for "James", I either did not answer or, as we got older, you anticipated the awkward interruption that would occur when I corrected the mistake. Sometimes, teachers would ask you if I was telling the truth. Other times teachers would have a mindless discussion with everyone to make sure that they heard me correctly. In kindergarten, teachers commonly marked me absent because I didn't realize I was a "James". A few years later, teachers openly wondered about my parents. By high school, everyone knew they were crazy.

However, another reason you might remember me as "Eric" is simpler: Many of you noticed that I misspelled it. Some of you had asked why I did that, but I didn't have an answer. I didn't mean to misspell it. I spelled it the way my parents misspelled it.

I was named "James" after my American grandfather. He was a chronic gambler and, according to one aunt, he was always drunk, taking some kind of drugs, driving into Gardena, other parts of L.A. or going out to Vegas where he would play poker, bet on boxing matches, watch horse racing or scheme seedy endeavors. In spite of this, though, my parents decided that, on balance, "James" was the best name for me when I was born in 1967.

Those were heady times, the late 1960s, but as times changed, and perhaps as everyone sobered up for NASA rocket launches, and as time pressed slightly into 1968 or '69, my parents realized their mistake and changed their minds. So, despite having seven or eight months in '67 to thoroughly consider their name choice, and write it onto my birth certificate, they reversed course and went with my middle name. I was always "Eric" as far as I remember. Never a "James".

My father rarely spoke but one time he said that my middle name came from a young German man who helped take care of him when he was little. I assumed that meant he knew someone named "Eric" but my father never said more about it. After he died, his sister wrote a long, thoughtful letter in English about their childhoods. It seems this mysterious German man was possibly named "Frederich".

My aunt, in her old age, remembered that during World War II, my father lived with a small family at a famous little estate in the countryside in eastern Prussia. I eventually found a historical website that listed the various men who had inherited the property before the communists took over in 1945. The most recent men were a father and son, both named "Frederich", if I recall.

I imagine my father removed the Fred-part knowing that Americans always shorten names, which, whether in a full-length or a shortened American form would have made me neither a "James" nor an

"Eric". Regardless of how he chose my middle name, he spelled it as "Erich", adding the 'h' in the German tradition. So, between being named after a wretched grandfather "James", and having a decent, although mysterious middle name-sake, my parents began calling me Erich using the American pronunciation. This is why, to this day, I misspell it.

My Transition

As many of you must feel in your joints and minds, our physical and mental resilience is diminishing. I am old and tired now. I cannot walk on roofs or climb the maple tree with the same lack of sense. Gravity works harder the higher I go. In fact, dangling 40 or 50 feet above the ground cutting tree branches helped me realize that Heaven does not need to be much higher. The transition from drudgery to *Paradise* would be quite gentle, too. Hanging any lower, though, I'd probably be too close to traffic. Eternity lasts too long to deal with traffic.

My thoughts go slower, too. In recent years, I began regularly introducing myself as "James" whenever meeting new neighbors or attending my children's school activities. This was supposed to keep things simple and be consistent with my driver's license, bank statements, PTA forms, and all other legal facets of my life. It also marked what was supposed to be the beginning of my special trans journey.

It's so sad. I was hoping to fix my bruised psyche but two things got in the way. First, we all remember what Buckaroo Banzai said: "Wherever you go…there you are." So true. This is so true. Take a moment. Sip your coffee, suck your ginger mint that is supposed to fix your blood balance, and reflect on that old, wise, memory. I can hear you echoing agreement: No matter how hard we try, we will never be able to take the "i" out of *ego*. And, secondly, heartbreakingly, and more sadly, everyone told me to stop misbehaving because they had already adjusted to the misspelled form of "Eric". The nerve! But I listened. And I re-reverted to "Erich"…again…to avoid trouble. People were so abrupt about it. Some of them challenged me like I was a child…again. I was so discriminated against you'd think I was homosexual…

My pronouns never changed, though. Pronoun flipping was never part of my transition, so the re-reversion back to "Erich" was barely noteworthy even among my trans-followers and the trans-vegans. You might not know what a trans-vegan is. They are not transvestites. They are former vegetarians who created a splinter organization called the "trans-associated vegan support group", which they simplified to *trans-vegans* to help their branding. Apparently, they are well-liked by transvestites because, as they say, vegan "cheese" doesn't taste funny like the meaty, fishy or eggy kinds. I don't know if that last part is true, though. I suspect that vegan Macaroni and "cheese" tastes just fine. I'm not against it, in principle. At any rate, trans-vegans didn't voice any concerns about my name change, or my preferred unchanged pronouns or my limited "cheese" repertoire. Everyone was politely quiet about the whole thing.

Most people near me, vegan or not, probably appreciate the consistency in my pronouns. I don't know if "Mister" is a pronoun, but if it is, I'd prefer to begin using it. Unfortunately, I believe I burned too many bridges with the various name-flipping fiascos over the years. But it hurts my feelings that nobody calls me "Mr. Keller" even though I strongly identify with it. It's such a shame.

If people around me were patient, empathetic[WTF] and sympathetic enough to help me make headway through my identity struggles, I would have re-reverted to "Erich" as a technicality but required everyone to call me, "Mr. Keller" in practice. This would have been an important step in my bi-trans-name-flipping mid-life breakdown assessment (which is possibly something Scientologists pay to do). But, I'm just too darned considerate. And, had I undertaken such a re-reversion step, no matter how therapeutic for me, everyone would have probably begun linking profane verbs, adverbs and adjectives to my various names, and maybe profane nouns as well. Literate sons-of bitches can be annoying, especially when they use fucking-hyphens incorrectly.

... ...

The Current me

Therefore, from my name-flipping experiences, you can see that there is a point where transvestite "decency-phobes" or the "anti-normals" cross lines with pronoun flipping that oppress and discriminate against old people like you and me who do not have enough mental faculties whirling in "our" brains to jump, crawl, roll, dig, hide, fly or simply piss on pronoun attackers as "we" try to avoid the ridiculous obstacles that the various fairies, freaks and maggots (the three F's) set up to foist on unsuspecting, yet well-aged, decent-enough old folks. And, just because "we" exist, does not mean the three F's must soil themselves and post the pictures on Twit-shit, Snap-shit, Insta-shit or some other brown cloud. Some movements should remain private. And, dammit, the Brucey Jenners should let me eat my apple pie in peace. Or is it custard tonight?

Anyway, that was the extent of my trans pronoun-flipping bull-nonsense endeavor. It's a head-scratcher, though. Such little empathy all around.

... ...

In the 1990s, a coworker said that I should write a book about how to make friends. He said, "Written by Eric, no James, no J. E.," sigh, "James E., J. Eric, no," sigh again, "James Eric Keller, with an ay'tch almost in the exact, God damned middle."

I said, "I think that would piss people off."

"It's pissing me off right now," he said.

I said, "I'd have to interview you for that book."

He used *shit* and *fuck-it* in an expressive sentence, then with a long, slow, exasperated exhale he said, "Duude, you could have spared the whoole world like 20 years ago if you had just gone with *James*."

I think we went to lunch after that.

The German Side

I never met my German grandparents. But a few years ago, during the COVID quarantine, I took a DNA test and began working on my family tree, which became a surprisingly interesting hobby. At the time, I knew practically nothing about my history. I vaguely knew that my German grandfather, Ludwig, had abandoned his family during World War II, making him little better than my American grandfather, James.

I vaguely knew that my German grandmother spent a few years packing and moving her five children across Germany to avoid British bombings on one side and to dodge the approaching Russians from the other. By 1943, one of my uncles turned 18 years old, and was immediately sent to fight in France. My father and the rest of his siblings remained disbursed among relatives and acquaintances in eastern Germany.

In time, the Russian army began pushing through Poland, so my aunt, who was 16 or 17 yrs old, convinced her mother that they needed to leave. Racial politics and other circumstances (like money, food and physical strength) and the overarching control of roads & traffic by the German military, forced my family to sneak west. On foot.

German civilians were not allowed to travel because the army had to keep roads clear for rapid deployments of troops and weapons. To make things more complicated, my young father and his siblings were living in different places across the countryside, so my grandmother and aunt had to quietly conspire to convince the brothers to sneak out of their different homes and meet at a certain place, on a certain evening, at a certain time.

My aunt made it sound very stressful as she and her mother waited that evening on the street corner of an eastern city (I forget which) for each boy to arrive. When they were together, and as the curfew was approaching, they began making their way west, hoping that the police would not stop them. By January 1945, they finally arrived in Dresden but getting there had some extra hardships that my aunt didn't write or speak much about. Because of this, the following description is fragmented.

Prior to reaching Dresden, my aunt had flagged down a west-bound train near Czechoslovakia. It was carrying German men and supplies but I don't know if they were going away from the fighting or redirecting to some other place to continue fighting. Her mother and brothers hid in a snowbank while she negotiated with the conductor.

In the 1980s, my father once said that you can flag down a train in the pitch dark using one cigarette. I asked, "How can you use one cigarette?" He explained that train conductors are taught to stop when they see a swinging light. "It's a universal sign that the tracks are out ahead." He didn't tell me more, but after reading my aunt's letter in the 1990s, I imagined she had to madly puff on a cigarette to keep it glowing while swinging it back-and-forth standing on snow-covered rails…and obviously, in the darkness.

Around 1994, she told me that after the train stopped, men shouted at her and argued until they saw the little boys. They finally let my relatives climb aboard because one of my uncles was a toddler. She also bribed the men with cigarettes. She sounded proud or surprised that she had been smart enough to gather boxes of cigarettes while in Silesia, and that she had been strong or stubborn enough to carry them in spite of helping to carry her littlest brother.

Shortly after the train began moving, presumably going towards Dresden, the conductor stopped again, this time to let my family off. The train had been redirected to Prague. So, my grandmother and her children were walking again; this time without boxes of cigarettes.

My three-year-old uncle had been sick on the trip, so when they reached Dresden, my grandmother arranged for her other children, including my father, to attend the local schools to allow time for her little boy to recover. Also, they needed rest, food and shelter. They had found one of my dad's school teachers from the East who had likewise escaped and ended up in Dresden. She had family in the city, so my relatives were able to squeeze in with them.

Although Dresden was safely in the middle of Germany, (I think it was the only big city that hadn't been bombed), it was crowded with German civilians trying to flee Russians in the east and avoid Americans in the west. Coincidentally, my relatives arrived when American planes began dropping leaflets across the area warning of a future bombardment. A few weeks later, Dresden was bombed into the stone age.

In the 1990s, my aunt said that she and her brothers departed the city on a crowded train the day the bombing began. In the 1970s or '80s, my father once plainly mentioned that when he was small, he looked up and the sky seemed to be made of metal. I asked, "From falling bombs?" He said, "No, from so many planes flying next to each other. It was hard to believe," he said, "that anyone could build so many and that they could fit up there at the same time."

Anyway, shortly after their train left Dresden, and they were out of harm's way, my grandmother and her children got off and began walking again. This time, she had learned that the Dresden train would turn south to Munich and she didn't want to go deep into Bavaria. Bavarian Germans are not nice to non-Bavarian Germans. My grandmother and her children ended up walking through the northern fringes of Bavaria until they found a tiny village covered in snow near a bend in a river. It had five or six old houses.

An ancient woman lived there among the few farmers. Everyone called her Tanta Anna, and her body was bent by arthritis. Tanta Anna let my relatives live with her for the final months of the war. My aunt wrote that life was as primitive as caveman times: no electricity, no piped water, no beds or blankets, and they had to make and gather everything to live. "You can't believe people went to bed hungry, got up the next morning hungry and started working." They remained there for several years. My grandmother died within a few more years.

Around April 1945, my dad turned 10 years old just as Americans arrived at the village with tanks and other heavy equipment. My aunt said everyone was terrified except for him. Guns were still blazing or were still hot, and she had to hug and hold him because he kept saying that he wanted to go out and talk to the Americans. It was late in an evening, and she had to watch him all night to make sure he didn't sneak out.

I once saw an interview of a Netherlander woman who had lived under German occupation for many years. She said when she saw British and American paratroopers floating down one sunny day in September 1944, it was like seeing Angels from Heavan coming to rescue her. I wonder if my father felt the same with the arrival of American troops.

As time passed, and as the war quieted down, some of the soldiers taught my dad how to kill fish by dropping hand grenades into the nearby river. He also learned to speak, read and write *American* instead of British English. I think the Americans knew that my relatives were not welcomed in the Bavarian community so my dad and his brothers seemed to be welcomed among the soldiers. Americans were known for their fairness. So, with an ample supply of freshly killed fish, my relatives were able to barter with local farmers for milk, bread and meat.

When the Americans forced the community to disarm, the entire region began turning in weapons. From this, my father once mentioned that he had stockpiled a lot of unexploded bombs, gunpowder and other ordinance that he dragged to a clump of trees in the woods near the river where he was able to accumulate boxes of grenades stacked on top of other contraband. Once in the early 1980s, he causally said something like, "If it had all exploded, someone was going to be in trouble."

American soldiers didn't stop him. Can you imagine a 10-year-old boy dragging a large, heavy box of grenades across the mud and a couple of American GIs saying, "Hey, kid. Let us help you with that."

When he was older, he volunteered for the US Army which is how he got his green card to immigrate to the United States. In the Army, he helped illiterate Americans write letters home and he would read letters to them that they had received. My aunt said that my father was surprised that Americans were so poorly educated even though they were from this rich, powerful country.

Because he was well-spoken, literate, and bilingual, he was transferred into Army Intelligence and deployed back to Germany where he worked for a long time until his commander discovered that he was not a US citizen. Foreign volunteers were not allowed in those intelligence roles.

After he got out of the service, he lived in Boston then moved to Los Angeles. I was born and raised in Southern California. My German grandmother died in 1950, when my father was in his mid-teens. Her ex-husband, my grandfather, died in 1979 but I never met him. A distant cousin of mine had once said that the old Keller was "ein schlectes Mann."

The American Side

My American grandparents lived in the same neighborhood as I did by Orangeview Junior High School, for those of you who went there. My American grandmother was very nice. She was my favorite relative because she was the only person who regularly spoke to me using polite sentences. She was a business owner. Her printing shop was in Los Angeles which she ran from about 1960 to the early 1990s. She had told me that she had been part of other businesses prior to 1960 in and outside of California, like in Florida, Texas, Illinois and a variety of other places. But, 1960 is about the time she and her children were able to settle in one place. She was born either in Oklahoma or Arkansas in the 1920s. I forget which place. I met her parents a few times in the 1980s when they were living in Arkansas.

My grandmother admired her father. She said things like, "He was a man of his word," and "His word was his bond." and "If he shook your hand, he meant it." She remembered traveling with him when she was a little girl while he looked for work. When Franklin Roosevelt's New Deal programs began in the early 1930s, she told me that she saw how lives were improved. It raised men's spirits and gave them pride, she said. As conservative as she was, she was a loyal Democrat. This had some limits, however. Towards the end of her life she said, "You know Erich, I am still going to vote for the Democrats, but I have to hold my nose when I go into the voting booth." Her parents were also Democrats.

As much as she admired her father, she had no love for her mother. She disliked her mother as much as she hated life in the countryside. Her mother believed girls wasted time in school. Girls needed to learn to be housewives. In contrast, my grandmother, as a little girl, enjoyed school very much. She said when she was three or four, her father would let her wander to a school house where she sat outside on a wooden step while he worked nearby. She would listen to the indoor lessons, and as time passed, older girls came outside to teach her to read and write simple words. As she got older, she looked forward to learning more but she had a fractious relationship with her mother. Apparently, my great-grandmother would lock her husband outside some evenings when he came home a little drunk. My grandmother would climb outside and sit with him on the porch. He always brought her a little snack, like toffee or something she called a "chicken-in-a-biscuit".

In the winter of 1944, when her future husband James arrived with a lot of mafia families, she said, "He was my ticket out." She and several of her relatives later told me that during winters, Chicago crime families traveled to Hot Springs to gamble in the warm weather. In the early 1980s, a year or two after my grandfather had died (of old age), my grandmother and I were standing near one of her printing presses. During a quiet moment, she pleasantly said, "I don't know how he survived for so long, but for some reason, none of those families tried very hard to kill him."

By the COVID era, electronic family trees were easily accessible. I entered the names of my American grandparents, and within a day or two, the automated system had plugged me into many family trees that overlapped and branched with my Arkansas relatives. In some cases, these records went backwards for centuries, twisting along lines generally leading to Britain or Switzerland. This worked only for my American grandmother. Nothing came up for her husband. Later, I found James' prison records from San Quentin. He had been born and raised in California, of all places, but by the 1930s, when so many people across the US were trying to get to California, he got out of prison and made his way east to Chicago…

…as opportunities permitted.

Chapter 2

Inspiration & Pride

My grandmother had many jokes about pride. One involved a preacher who got caught outside in a rain storm. As water levels rose, and as he prayed for Salvation, four different good Samaritans separately offered to rescue him but he refused each time. After he drowned and learned he was being sent to Hell, he proclaimed, "I had faith, Lord! Why am I damned?" God rumbled, "First, I sent a four-wheel drive truck, then a canoe, a boat and finally a helicopter. All you had to do was get in one of them."

My extensive family tree raises the question whether any of my relatives contributed to historical events like the American Revolution, or whether I am related to anyone famous. Funnily…I like the word funnily…the short answer is no, I do not have famous relatives. A few distant relatives were veterans of the American Revolution but without distinction. In one case, a great great great (x5 or x6) grandfather was sought for desertion. That's not too good. But among the numerous branches, it was nice to find connections that overlapped with textbook history.

As I learned more about my ancestors, I realized that new information can dent pride, but I also recognized that details from within a family usually depict the same historical dynamics that happened at higher levels of world events. The same acrimony, pride and celebration that affect a small family will similarly affect nations.

However, at the level of family connections, when we do not have important ancestors, there is a desire to associate with a *group, place* or an *event*. For example, in first or second grade, boys around me on the playground suddenly began bragging that they were Irish. They were very excited about this. For some reason, they had decided that this was a status symbol that embodied a right to play together during recess. One of my friends ran up to me and loudly asked, "Erich! Are you Irish, too?!!" I said, "I don't know!" He said, "Do you *want* to be Irish?" I said, "Ok*!*" Then he turned and shouted to the other boys, "Erich is Irish, too!"…with much rejoicing. Yet, funnily enough, in Southern California in the early 1970s, about half of my schoolmates were brown or Asian. But on that day, we were all Irish together.

We quickly and completely forgot about being Irish but during that moment on the playground, it seemed correct to go along with the general attitude. Later, around that time, I asked my mom if we were Irish, she said no. When my father got home, I asked him. He gave me a questioning glance then said no. I suppose most of the boys did the same thing, which is probably why the whole issue was quietly dropped. Still, it seems like a good general life experience.

This little experience helps explain why nationalism and royalty become important to some people. In dysfunctional cultures, monarchy is a national obsession. The king and queen are considered to be heavenly embodiments of the nation, sitting on clouds or thrones, surrounded by opulence, never having to wipe themselves because God coated their asses with Teflon. And, according to most of these royal traditions, in some manner-or-other, across human civilizations, the King, with inspired pride and confidence reaches into his Queen's royal vagina, pulls out their royal realm, and proclaims, "By Jove! Good job, Dear," as he clears his throat in a fancy way. Cultural and civic pride are important, just like having fun during recesses. In a healthy culture, however, pride should not be cartoonish. We don't have royalty in the United States.

I decided to cut down the size of this next paragraph. It digressed into movies and music from the 1970s and 1980s focusing on music by John Williams and movies by Stephen Spielberg. Then I thought, If I can't spell Speilberg's name correctly, then I should drop the whole thing. Maybe I was thinking of Steven King and got them mixed up.

Like our children, we probably lived through earlier times without marking events, and we probably exaggerated the importance of unimportant things. For example, a few years after we graduated when the Berlin Wall came down in 1989, we knew this was remarkable but when oil prices were fifteen bucks a barrel throughout the earlier 1980s, we paid no attention, probably relieved the crazy Muslims of the 1970s had faded away. We didn't realize that oil prices combined with President Reagan's attitude towards evil empires had defanged the Middle East and bankrupted the godless communists of Russia. This detachment is why history lessons feel impractical.

When taught correctly, history is wisdom. Wisdom helps us navigate the present and predict the future, which helps us protect children. This is why wisdom has value. Making history learnable, though, is tricky. Lessons must be entertaining to the point of appearing superficial, especially for children. But since inspiration and pride are forms of entertainment, we must be careful because we do not want to manipulate children. Entertainment, you see, can be very helpful for building friendships and community cohesiveness but it can be used to degrade wisdom…depending on how it is used.

For example, in the 1990s, my grandmother along with one of my aunts and a young cousin went to San Francisco for a week. My aunt said she thought it would be a nice vacation. They saw the Golden Gate Bridge, went to the big green park by the bridge, rode streetcars, and generally were tourists. They said the weather was uncharacteristically nice.

Among the sites that they encountered was a gay pride parade. This was accidental. And consequently, without much shame or hesitation, my grandmother removed her windbreaker and wrapped it over her head.

My aunt asked, "Mom, what are you doing?!"

My grandmother said, "I don't want these TV cameras showing my face on the news tonight."

My cousin said, "Nan, stop doing that and put on your coat."

My grandmother refused.

Now. My point: many months after this event, my aunt says to me, "Erich, I'm all in favor of equality. If anyone has to go through managing their feelings in a society that discriminates against them, then I am completely understanding towards that…But this parade was not about homosexuality. The entire parade had naked men swinging their private parts in public. This was not celebrating equality. They were just putting on a sex show in public. Why do they do that?"

I had no answer. But my grandmother looked at me, and calmly said, "I still think I made the right decision. I didn't want any of my friends to see me on TV and wonder why I was at that parade."

I made some mental notes about this and probably did not say much.

You see, this is where gay pride degenerated. Sin can be partly defined by where you put a penis. But sin is forgivable. It can be temporary and the behavior can be correctable. Abomination, on the other hand, is obsession. Abomination is addiction. It leads to a permanence that is, at its heart, anti-decent. It is a selfishness that denies decency among and within the community. Cain would spread this among children. Abomination can also be called damnation, at least after death arrives. In life, it's simply degenerate.

For the Class of 1985

It is wise for heterosexuals to make allowances to allow people to be free but it is not wise to allow people to degrade us sexually. Homosexual men will say that they were misbehaving because they had been repressed. Yet, I disagree because if they had such freedoms decades or centuries earlier, they would have almost certainly behaved the same way except that by the 1990s, they would have evolved to have sex with animals during the parades.

If you disagree, let me remind you that HIV evolved from a fragile, poorly contagious monkey virus. And later, in the 2000s, Monkeypox appeared in gay men the microsecond after HIV drugs allowed men to get on with having more degenerate sex...apparently with monkeys. Therefore, these homosexual men in the 1990s era San Francisco were not celebrating equality. They built entertainment around sex, which degenerated into excessive pride. And the excessive pride set the stage for greater degeneration with animal sex. Bam! Call me toxic.

I have heard people say that Christianity teaches us that sex is bad. This is not true. Cavemen and cavewomen had the same brains and abilities to observe the world as we have. They almost certainly observed that if a woman has sex too often, she will either die, her child or children will be born dead or she will not be able to have children.

Cave-people don't need Jesus to explain this to them. They will observe the effects and link hypersexual behavior with poor health. That is all. You might call this superstition but this is almost certainly a reason that across many cultures excessive sex is considered to be a bad lesson for young children.

Therefore, the gay parade of the 1990s was more likely a public display of exercising freedom to groom & recruit children rather than an effort to simply gain social acceptance from the heterosexual world.

You see, if we capitulate and allow hypersexual men to do whatever they want wherever they desire to do it, they would not bring some kind of

41

Utopian existence. They would simply become tyrants and foist excuses to oppress anyone they dislike – like calling someone *toxic* instead of calling them a dirty Jew, nigger or something else. They are not heavenly people speaking with God's voice. They are liars. Even Vladimir Lenin, the godless communist pig that he was, was honest about his political goals: he wanted communists to take power so factory workers could be the new oppressors.

--

This progression from wisdom to entertainment to pride and degeneration is not new. In the 1750s, Benjamin Franklin observed (and, a hundred years earlier, John Milton similarly alluded to it in 1642), that people, particularly men, were easily swayed by entertainment. When people believed they have a bond through social events like plays, music or religious revivals, then community cohesiveness improved, which made governing easier. Therefore, community leaders recognized very early on that entertainment can be used to fuel pride to push men along a chosen political path. Women are not better than men in this regard; it was simply a male dominated world back then.

Without community pride, it is difficult to lead men. Actually, it's impossible. Leadership requires working towards a symbol that the community rallies behind. The stronger the loyalty to that symbol, the easier it is to lead. Hence, dramatic things like protecting our children, going to war, having Space Races, competing in sports, singing, dancing, acting, and so forth are tools used to promote either heroism or at least covetous desire (e.g., politics, hypersexualism, etc.), which strengthens loyalty. Even when the stories are exaggerated or flatly dishonest, as long as actors and actresses do a good job, the audience will accept fictional courage. When an audience fawns puppets, the worship reinforces pride. We become inspired.

Strong emotional ties create social status and acceptance, and, if pride is strong enough, people believe that they are superior to others because of their association (with a team, with an actor or some other famous face) allows the fan to claim that their God, their dancer, athlete or favorite doctor is better than yours; they feel smarter, cleaner, prettier by singing praises for someone else... They have a sense of belonging even though they buy their membership.

Therefore, we value family and national histories that give us emotional strength and reassure us that we have value. How we *feel* about these histories, however, is seismically different from how we should *study* them. For example, this distinction is why WOKE history lessons can be immoral. When any lesson is structured to uplift one religion, one skin color, or a group of men over another to make them *feel* reassured and valued, then the lessons are dishonest. They are propaganda. WOKE history runs this risk by possibly propagandizing Black history hoping to uplift the spirits of one group of students. Accurate history lessons will hold skin color and religion in a correct context. This balance imparts value. Everything else is commentary. Commentary is nagging. Nagging is disrespectful.

Another example, but in contrast to WOKE-ism: the reason English history is important in the United States is not because we speak English or because the US revolted against Britain but because England has 1100 years of written history covering political growth, population growth, exports & imports, international negotiations & war, religious turmoil, evolution of common law, English law, legal precedent, and treason & treachery; all of which are well-documented in some written form in England. Skin color and language have nothing to do with the historical value of that mass of information.

If Japan had formed the United States and relegated all Europeans and Africans to slavery, we'd still be studying English history in North

America because the scientific, industrial and agricultural revolutions of Earth largely began in England around the 1600s onward. The racist elements of English history arise only when Englanders, the Britons, try to explain why they are better than brown people. Their quick but incorrect answer is racist – they say they are superior to all comers even better than the stupid Irish.

The true reason that England was able to become the center of recorded modern history is because it is an island at the fringe northern reach of Europe but not frozen over with glaciers. Also, a thousand years ago, it had good farmland, reasonably high food production, a lot of mineral wealth including a variety of metals along with coal & iron, and after the 1580s, it was largely insulated from the chaos of waring Catholics who spread death and disease across Europe and South America. England had resources, a strong population, social resilience and at least three written languages (Latin, French and English) for over 1000 years. These ingredients made England one of the more productive locations on Earth, and it makes the organized progression of its history important. Skin color is irrelevant.

Today, England still uses its history to bring imaginary pride to British subjects. Beyond England, though, this same type of pride exists in all cultures for religious, political, athletic and all other social matters. Depending on the person's confidence or insecurity, we gravitate towards histories and legends that justify why our team is better than yours to make you feel inferior for not being a member, and maybe try to convince you to join. Or at least, we hope you will desire to join. You might have the wrong family name or something, which would make you unwelcomed but you should still wish to be part of our group.

Family histories, therefore, can be double-edged swords. When populated with diverse relatives, who are depicted accurately, such stories when told well can impart much wisdom, but the same stories can be boring and uninteresting because they link us to things that require careful thought or are embarrassing and offensive.

Glaringly dysfunctional family histories revolt us; we want to escape the past even when that means walking into an insecure future. My American grandmother, for example, felt trapped by a network of relatives. She resented the restrictions and rebelled. And though her family's social bonds would have guaranteed her a secure future, she decided to escape with a convicted felon to seek opportunities elsewhere in the country.

Broader histories beyond our immediate families which foster nationalism & pride, help highlight common ties across the nation to shield us from our dysfunctional pasts. However, to be wise, we must each realize that no matter how respectful and truthful the storyteller, we will gravitate towards the parts of the stories that are most important to each of us, which tempts us to create tailored or sanitized versions of the same events…creating possibly misleading, and inaccurate narratives to inspire us. This can be manipulative.

Feminism

Ignoring hypersexuals and crazy politicians, another example of misleading historical narratives is American feminism. Feminism is supposed to represent a shared sisterhood. Ideally, this is important for everyone. However, US and non-US feminists are rarely on the same page. Why? In other countries, women mainly target the traditional themes of equal access to education, professional development and guaranteed respect from the community.

Decent men and women want to ensure everyone can have equal access to living in clean, safe, prosperous communities where women and men can apply themselves and achieve the same rewards as anyone doing equivalent work. We want men and women to have equal rights under the law to own property and to be able to conduct themselves in public and private according to their desires provided they are good, fair members of society. If they are not decent, then they lose their freedom and lose their property. In light of this, we do not want one group to arbitrarily hold another group in servitude. Therefore, neither women nor men should teach boys and girls that one sex is superior to the other. Such lessons chain children to whichever propaganda they hear at the youngest age. It's a type of slavery.

My grandmother was pretty much of the "foreign" camp. She was friendly and sociable with men and women in business and political communities. She enjoyed talking and learning about people, and to some extent, to my discomfort, she was willing to politely discuss abortion or other similar uncomfortable things. She did this well, though. Aside from this book, I avoid political and religious discussions but my grandmother confidently navigated these topics while remaining thoughtful and considerate towards opposing opinions.

She didn't go for the jugular. She made the other person feel at ease as she worked up and around a topic. She gauged the situation like an easygoing vegetarian tiger studying its prey and politely regretting that it was not allowed to kill it. She found joy in these discussions. She did not debate in a typical American way, though. She spoke, asked and listened. She was polite. You can't offend your customers when they arrive to pay for their business cards.

When asked about her positions or opinions, she typically answered with allegorical stories, like about her father looking for work or her husband dodging gambling debts. In spite of the subject matter, she avoided controversy. I don't know how to accurately describe her. She was able to depict the things that made her tick without burdening the listener. She wasn't perfect but she could craft a fair balance and know when to back-off, at least around me.

This is different from most people who desperately want to be heard and desperately want to "win" the argument, to score a point and protect their egos. She wasn't like a typical, noisy American. Most American feminists argue from theory. My grandmother wasn't a feminist. She said, "I never had the time because I always had to work."

If American feminism is about equality, then why is it so complicated? American feminists do not seem to seek basic fairness anymore. Everyone wants to compete and score. They want to be celebrated. But consequently, there is too much diversity among *feminist* topics. These topics become obnoxious because they have little merit and sound like never-ending complaints: "Tell us what makes you angry, then we'll ask you to donate & subscribe."

Recently there was humorous outrage by some American women complaining that professional female athletes are paid much less than professional male athletes. Linking the claim to men was unfounded, however. Professional ice skating and other dance-related sports almost certainly pay women better than male-equivalent performers. It's not rocket science. Ticket sales & merchandising define profits.

Women's football and basketball? Americans do not worship those events therefore, the female athletes get paid little. Feminists soiled themselves about evil businessmen even though, as far as I can tell, men, in general, did nothing wrong.

Because feminism is one big sisterhood, however, the rational, good feminists remained quiet instead of smacking down the indecency. And, I doubt the complaining side ever stepped back from their outrage to give a full-throated explanation for why she/they could not understand simple fan-based economics in the first place.

I like to imagine that noise from complaining women is only temporary and will diminish, but at the time, I had two small children being influenced by the dishonesty permeating into schools. Shame on the bad feminists. Shame on the good ones. Substance seems to be lacking from these crazy women who believe they represent 50% of human life. And when the good, decent feminists do not instantly attack the bad ones, the world wonders if the good feminists are as numerous as we wish.

Post-1970, American feminism became wealthy, but like modern-day politics, nobody has humble social goals anymore. *"That government is best, which governs least,"* is long gone. Nowadays, the social influencer makes noise to raise spontaneous money, promising that Hell is around one corner and Utopia is around the other. Buy an EV today. Save the world! Hate men to help women!

This means the intellectual side of American feminism, the side seeking social and professional fairness has been eclipsed by a princessy self-righteousness rooted in the wealth of their club. Everything centers on immediacy: Smash LIKE, Subscribe, hit-the-bell, go-to-hell, go to our Patreon page…your donation is inspiring…but don't forget, if boys or men have ever upset you, set up your never-ending subscription today! It's the greatest fan-driver in history…right next to blaming Jews and Blacks for all the other problems.

When my grandmother was a baby in the 1920s, an advertising man named Edward Bernays convinced feminists that they could achieve power and influence by smoking cigarettes. And, he succeeded. He helped tobacco companies open the women's market. He called cigarettes, "Torches of Freedom", which inspired women to suck proudly. Once you make people feel they are part of a group, you can convince them to believe anything. *Addiction* and *Subscription* are the same.

Bernays reasoned that you can rarely convince individuals to change their behavior but if you appeal to a group, the social angst reverberates so deeply in their vaginas, that it replaces individualism with a herd mentality. That herd mentality is so intense that individual thinking becomes taboo. Group loyalty is the priority. (Men behave similarly but without the reverberating vagina part.)

Bernays showed that when a group is manipulated from the outside, by an influencer like a "Wizard of Oz" who pulls levers to introduce an absurd belief, the social pressure inside the group amplifies the pitch while degrading individualism until everyone teeters and totters on a knife-edge facing a humiliating tip one way or another. They get trapped into thinking they cannot go back and, and on balance, they opt to risk an uncertain future to save their pride. Consequently, they prefer to tip towards uncertainty. This is identical to my grandmother's position in Arkansas back in the 1920s and into the 1940s.

Before moving on and picking on men, it's worth noting, I think, that American feminism is an abomination because of two qualities: First, the organization is constantly refining and legally bolstering a fictional form of chivalry, which they foist onto boys even though the code is not humanly achievable. These same women will cry and bemoan photoshopping and other commercialized tools used to manipulate little girls to reach unattainable levels of beauty, but the same feminists foist nearly identical impossible standards on little boys. Then many of these bitches have the nerve to act surprised when autism spiked in little boys in the 1990s (when sexual harassment complaints exploded in the US). In truth, women simply could not tolerate that men existed, and toddler boys possibly reacted to this degrading noise.

Second, feminists use courts to establish and reinforce judicial prejudice defending the woman's right to behave almost any way she wishes with little liability. Both the foisted chivalry and legal cover burden boys with an abundance of grinding shame that decent American men would never dump onto little girls. Yet, both acts have become institutionalized so that changing these attitudes would be like removing fluoride from drinking water. Everyone would say, *"You can't do that! Can you?"*

Therefore, in case you missed it, let me reiterate that decent people would never treat little girls with the same extensive hatred that American feminists have foisted onto little boys. This type of hypocrisy is not limited to hypersexual and bitchy feminist arguments, but it is a good, emotionally-charged way of jamming my finger into your crack to get your attention. As far as I can tell, modern-day American feminists preach religious damnation of the male half of society while shaming anyone who voices fairness.

In June 1900, Theodore Roosevelt wrote, "At times a man must cut loose from his associates and stand alone for a great cause." Do you think American women, feminist or not, have the moral strength to defend this country beyond their immediate tribes? Such stamina and commitment are supposed to make the United States great again. But by dividing ourselves among countless groups where the main action is defending corruption within our chosen tribalism is immature.

Let's recap: The entire reason you are in your civil or political group is because you believe it is better than other groups. Your group is supposed to carry your dreams of greatness, and light the way along a more prosperous path. So, stop the arrogant nonsense, and, when necessary, stand alone and be a decent person. Your team should make you stronger and better, not stupider. In 1910, Roosevelt also said that your actions should, "…add substantially to the sum of world achievement." Start adding. Stop detracting.

Man-ism

"...he made us understand that the same standard of clean living was demanded for the boys as for the girls; that what was wrong in a woman could not be right in a man."

T. Roosevelt, 1913

Men follow the same "feminist" pattern except they wish to celebrate strength and individualism. For example, Theodore Roosevelt said, "A just war is...better for a man's soul than the most prosperous peace." Amen. But it is probably more accurate to say that a just war does more for men who stayed home, avoided the fight and gained wealth and pride from the heroic, courageous men who suffered through the fighting. A *just war* becomes propaganda for the home front. A *just war* lets people break social boundaries to "get the job done", which brings a sense of liberation from dysfunctional bureaucracy and by static social rules.

At its heart, this manly desire to "get the job done" by breaking civil boundaries during war is attractive even to women because it brings opportunities to exercise our ability to make decisions, take action and contribute quickly and positively to our surroundings with fewer convoluted rules. We all want to be resourceful and industrious.

Yet, we each have a sixth sense to recognize highly dysfunctional situations in our childhoods even when we do not understand why we dislike them. This is why many boys want to go to war and why many girls want to be carried away by a mysterious stranger. We wish to be liberated from our overly controlling surroundings.

My grandmother, for example, broke with her family in Arkansas because of an instinctive desperation; to avoid in-breeding, if not from actual sex, then from incestuous social rules that excluded outsiders and stifled healthy intellectual growth. She had no opportunities to seek greener pastures, so, the only path available was to reject her parents and her extended family. Her behavior became a declaration of war. She became liberated from one situation but imprisoned by the tyranny of a different world.

From my grandmother's perspective, though, this change let her leave behind stale and restricted superstitions. War is not exciting for the killing and destruction but for the two opportunities that open to us: (1) it helps us escape our closed circumstances while (2) it justifies our misbehavior, and makes social changes appear to be forced upon us when we actually welcomed change.

War and violence between nations are the easiest dynamics to see and celebrate, because when heroes rise up and are crowned as our new idols, we see the American Dream play out. Family fortunes are tied to the fortunes of war. War opens doors that remain closed in peacetime. So, yes, a just war does a lot for us.

Man's desire to have high social status in a group and exhibit rugged leadership and rugged individualism at first seems to be completely opposite of American feminism, yet these qualities address nearly the same desires that women have: everyone wants to increase their social status & pride. The male ingredients are more hypocritical than the female side because social status and rugged individualism cancel each other. Thank God men are easier to understand.

On the whole, men are tipped towards competition. Women, on average, are more comfortable cooperating. This makes sense because if a woman gets sick while pregnant, for example, she can die or be permanently impaired. Collective knowledge for women, therefore, can be valuable for immediate survival. Such collective knowledge can become wisdom if it is organized well. On the other hand, it can be manipulated to encourage women to suck on Freedom Torches to look cool.

Therefore, feminists and their male opposition are equally dysfunctional, and in some regards are equally justified. The basic lesson is that Jesus did not fight the Jews or Romans. He opposed the hypocrites. He advocated the Golden Rule and said that we should practice what we preach. We have too much preaching and hypocrisy today.

Children-ism

When my son was a young teenager, I told him, "There are cultures in the world that teach girls that they are dirty and unwanted because someday they will menstruate. We would not imagine living among such primitive people and allowing them to influence your sister with such nonsense. Yet, in the US, for the past 50 or 60 years, American feminists have constantly criticized boys simply because boys were born. Most women do not seem to see that their social & emotional degradation of boys is identical to primitive cultures that degrade girls. We do not want girls or boys to be ashamed of existing. On the other hand, some American women know exactly what they are doing, which makes them equivalent to the cruelest of men; they enjoy humiliating boys. Who stands up against such bitches? Courts seem to protect them."

Decent people want children to grow up safely, become productive adults, do a good day's work and go to bed feeling that they did something worth doing. That final part of the day should not be spent foisting pride.

As adults, we need to face the end of the day decently because good behavior is an important ingredient for raising and protecting children and grandchildren. We do not want to celebrate or invite suffering, nor do we wish to ignore happiness. But at the same time, we should not live like a bunch of over-stimulated idiots who need to listen to three minutes of music to help us survive the next four minutes of life.

For the Class of 1985

The American "Feminist"

In one of her SUVs,
the trophy wife,
who has shoes galore,
and is an extravagant whore,
is driving to buy more shoes
at her favorite shoe store.
But she drives along with little glee,
as she desperately tries to flee,
from Church…
or Mass, whichever it be,
because she has some discomfort you see,
from not selling enough merch…
and by using her ass improperly.
Oh. She is doubly upset…
with the size and shape
of her costly boobies.

As her friends listen to three-and-a-half minutes of music…
…to help them survive on Earth four minutes more.
She says to the woman who sells her the shoes,
at the shoe store,
"Yes, it's a shame…
…but it's only a game…
…to see who is speedier…
…to tell God which bastards are greedier."
And, in her heart she wonders,
Whether *He* will stroke or strike her,
With another Holy Hemorrhoid,
Or a Heavenly…Meteor.

Chapter 3

Truthfulness

In the 1980s, I visited Arkansas with my grandmother. Her father was in his 80s. He spoke to me about many things. One of his stories was about when he retired. He was a mason. He said, "Some men, you get the feelin right away, that they'r reliable: you tell'em what ta do, an' later you check an' see they'r doin' it, an' you never have to worry about them ever again. Other men are lazy, so you gotta treat'em like dogs, cuz that's all they'r good fur. Some of 'em are White an' some are Black. Skin color don't make no difference." The next part made him teary. He said, "After I retired, some of the White men showed up here at the house an' offered my wife n me a collection of cash. They had gone to da bank n got fresh money ta hand ta us. En' they had nice, kind words to say about working under me. Then later, a group of Black men showed up. They had an old coffee can that they'd filled with coins. One said, "Mr. Plyler, we know'd you was fair all-a 'deese years, and 'dis is da best we could put togetha for you n Mrs. Plyler."

Back in California, I told this story to my parents and siblings. I recall not being sure if anyone was listening, but after I finished, my dad asked in a startled voice, "Who told you that!?" I said, "Grandpa Plyler." He said, "Oh." I said, "Why are you surprised?" He said, "Back in 1970 we visited Arkansas and went to a hospital after he had stomach surgery. When we got there, he was laying on a bed in the hall. Your grandmother asked him, "Dad, why are you laying out here?" He said, "Because I don't wanna share a room with no dirty [Blacks]."
In the blink of an eye, my father must have decided that he wasn't going to let the sanitized retirement story stand unchallenged. To my best recollection, though, my father never said the word, nigger.

-

Norman Maclean was an American author. In 1976, he published his book titled, "*A River Runs Through It*". In the 1990s, Robert Redford made the movie. Maclean's writing style is easy to assess because he published only three or four short stories. In spite of this, in some literary circles, he is considered a great American writer. I am not a well-trained writer, but Maclean is easier to read than Hemingway, Steinbeck and O. Henry. At the very least, you might remember we read *The Old Man and the Sea* (Hemingway), *The Pearl* (Steinbeck) and *The Gift of the Magi* (O. Henry) in our childhoods. Those stories all have some kind of deep anxiety woven into the narratives. Maclean did not do that.

Generally, Hemingway's characters have skin peeling emotional pain that often stems from rugged, apathetic unhappiness. Most of his characters seem to live in some kind of drunken cloud. It's very disorienting. His novels are very good, but his short stories can be hell. Immense mental preparation is needed to sit and read a Hemingway short story. I feel like his characters need to do behind-the-scenes interviews to help the reader find out what the hell they were doing.

Steinbeck is much easier to read than Hemingway but Steinbeck has too much morality. I can read Steinbeck straightaway but I am always distracted because a moral will smack me sooner or later.

O. Henry's stories are good but they make me nervous because I identify with his dirty scenes and veiled optimism. But his characters are so desperate, I find it exhausting to suffer with them.

All three writers seemed to torture their characters (or their readers).

Maclean, in contrast, has an old sincerity built into his writing that avoided character gimmicks. But he was very old when he first published anything; in his 70s, and he did not write much, which protects him from over-analysis and criticism.

In the introduction to his *River* book, Maclean stated something important about his role as a father. He wrote that his stories, "…[let] children know what kind of people their parents are or think they are or hope they are." If you randomly open a book and pick a paragraph or one sentence to ponder, you might see the architecture of it, especially if the writer is good. This sentence was one of those.

It progresses from 'rigid understanding' to 'optimistic perception' to 'imagination' of how we wish to be. It's an intellectual transformation; and the sentence is as important as anything he or anybody else on Earth across all times and languages has ever written. He concisely and respectfully defined the godly side of the human condition. We wish to be decent and truthful.

Like a sentence from the *Old Testament*, it gives us a mature perspective almost as high as *Providence*: telling us that rightness and wrongness require careful consideration. Regardless of how we interpret Maclean's actual intention, his sentence gave us a simple truth about ourselves and gave fair warning that his story was probably not as truthful as he would have liked. It's a novel. It's fiction. But truthfulness about thinking, hoping and wishing to convey his integrity as a father, son and brother strengthened the novel's value. Truth did not diminish its literary value.

Maclean's father said salvation comes from *Grace*, *Grace* comes from art, art comes from work, work is difficult. Our dilemma is that we each balance between past mistakes, while usually having too much pride which blurs wisdom. Wisdom has value because it can help our children move through life and into a prosperous or at least a safer future…

But, since wisdom comes with difficulty, and since memories fade, and since the art of thinking is difficult…Wisdom, if we ever grasp it, is always fleeting. Over time, your wisdom will be forgotten, and, consequently, children must rediscover it.

Working like a mule does not earn *Grace* or bring wisdom. Work must blend obligation and hope to become a correct kind of art. Therefore, wisdom and *Grace* can seem identical but the two are not the same, and having a connection between them is not always obvious or guaranteed.

For example, the very act of communicating a true story smears the original memory. Each retelling bends, twists and stretches the truth, which risks replacing the truth with something of lessor value. The ability to protect wisdom, therefore, comes with practice. Perfect retelling is not necessary. In fact, perfect retelling is not good because wisdom is not visible through the struggle and hurt. We find wisdom only after time allows us to sort through the mess, and after much of the hurt and struggle have subsided.

A sanitized story, therefore, like from my great grandfather, nurtures wisdom. He gave me a simple story that had both a little wisdom and some *Grace* but he chose to leave behind his racist side.

Maturity can bring wisdom. And since maturity can bring *Grace* then *Grace* and wisdom are more artistic accomplishment than simply the process of aging. And though the integrity of Maclean (the storyteller) cannot be quantified, it was a vital fuel that he (the writer) tried to defend to preserve his (the man's) self-respect. His manners and effort to communicate his story in the last stretch of his life, and his ornery stubbornness about not wanting to compromise his story for the Redford screenplay, conveyed the *value* of his art through his *Grace* which he harbored as a good writer and, I suspect, as a good man.

I suppose Maclean retained the essence of his story while protecting his true private memories. No matter how good the writer, as an old man, it was not possible for him to be as truthful as he preferred. Maclean seems to be touching on the same feeling I have when writing about my father's war experiences. We do not wish to be disrespectful. The act of telling a sensitive story, however, puts the truth precariously on the edge of inaccuracy, exaggeration and outright lying.

Writers wrestle with this type of dishonesty that can creep into anyone's writing. We naturally ignore or change things to satisfy the linear organization and rhythm of sentences and paragraphs. And, like my grandmother's social and debating skills, we can tailor stories to support some current political point out of respect for the people in our past, but we can also bend the truth to impress the reader or boost our pride at the expense of the same good people whom we tried to champion. You cannot get into Heaven by lying. The paths leading up that hill are steep and crowded with teams. Lying will not help. Once we tip into the practice of fabricating details, however, the temptation to continue along that path becomes an addiction. It never ends. Therefore, you should not focus on the author's truthfulness; truthfulness is always doubtful from a distance, but instead estimate his integrity and sincerity.

Had Maclean not acknowledged that his narrative had crossed-over into fiction, he would have died a liar. His truthfulness about being dishonest is a rugged maturity that ends up being the main lesson: his story tries to describe what he was like, or thought he was like or hoped that he was like. He was respectful to his audience and to his art, which embodied his integrity. We should all work to be like that.

As adults, we try to give depth to our beliefs but if we do this sloppily, we become shallow liars who say things only for pride and arrogance. Like I wrote in the Introduction, at my age and condition, I have little knowledge these days but I have not stepped away from my opinions. For most Americans, for some reason, it seems we cannot step back and say we tried to be impressive, hoped to be included, or wished to get a hug. Pride and social acceptance are powerful. We have to be careful how we approach both. We shouldn't try to be clever to cover our flaws and manipulate people. We should cleverly organize our beliefs.

I forget who, either John Milton or John Locke, in the 1600s, wrote something vaguely along the lines of, '*People have the moral abilities to sore nearly as high as Heaven and at other times dig nearly as deep as Hell*'. I lost the correct quote a long time ago. Sounds like Milton rather than Locke. But from it, it helps to define how we use pride: it can be used to inspire, which means we will always desire to exaggerate our strengths and downplay our weaknesses. We are not humble enough, which diminishes our willingness to learn and be decent. We always hope to meet Abel but we anticipate coming face-to-face with Cain.

I told my children that it's easier to be truthful. Lying can be easy at first. But when we have to cover things up, life becomes too difficult.

Mark Twain simply said, "*If you tell the truth, you don't have to remember anything.*"

Chapter 4

Snow, Ice and a Creek

When my son was very small, he sweetly asked, "Why is white rice white?" except he pronounced R's like W's so it sounded like, "Why is why-t why-ss why-t?" I opened my eyes and repeated his question. A gentle smile spread across his face, he blinked slowly and quietly said, "Yeah, why is it aw'ways white?" I eventually said, "It's another mystery of the universe." Like my pride.

When my son was little, before 2010, I commonly took him to various woods, creeks and nearby parks. He did not grow up watching TV although we watched Japanese "Romper Room" VHS videos on an old television that my dad gave me back in 1989. My son had a very quiet upbringing.

After he finished his first day at an American pre-school, and before I could ask him anything about his day, he smiled at me, his eyes sparkled, and the first thing out of his mouth was a triumphant, "I love girls!" and he began hopping with happy energy.

Around the time that he was beginning to have American friends, we had a rougher winter than usual. Maryland typically gets an inch of snow. But in 2009-10, we had a strange thunder snowstorm that knocked out electricity for at least a week, right before my daughter was born. It was a tornado or a snownado. I think the newspapers called it Snowmagedon. The storm had taken down phone poles, power lines and trees around my neighborhood and across the region. Some neighborhoods were without power for over a month. Our house remained above 50 deg F during the power outage, which was fine. We used blankets and wore layers of clothes. And, I regularly shoveled and shoveled snow.

On some particular day, shortly before or shortly after his sister was born, and after digging out of my driveway all morning, my son and I walked to a nearby park. I stomped through three feet of snow along the sidewalk so he could follow. He was just old enough to manage on his own and he had fun jumping from one of my foot prints to the next.

The park sits atop a hill surrounded by a small clump of woods that are surrounded by houses of our neighborhood. On the hill are swings. We dusted snow off of one of them, I lifted him, placed him snuggly on the seat with his winter clothing bulging around him, then began pushing. With each gentle pass, his short legs and boots gradually carved a trench in the snow beneath him. The day was sunny and peaceful. Nobody else was outdoors.

As any dad will do, in any weather, I continued pushing him higher and higher for the extra excitement it brings. At the high point of each push, he began playfully releasing and quickly snapping his grip back onto the swing to feel the momentary weightlessness before the downward arc. He was happily chatting and humming the whole time until, finally, both his mittens slipped and he tumbled backwards.

He fell in a disturbingly slow-motion way, landing head-first. It was a very high fall. He came to an abrupt stop with his head and upper body inserted into soft snow. I don't think he had time to kick his legs because in an eyeblink, I leapt and crawled over heaps of snow to get to him. I grabbed his boots, reached down into the snow and pulled him out, set him upright and sharply and aggressively barked, "Dude! Are you ok!"

They say a crying baby is a fairly healthy baby. He was crying when I got to him but he stopped abruptly when he heard my question, and the shape of his face changed as if he had licked a lemon. He convulsed with a quick laugh, stared up at me through the snow on his sunglasses then giggled as he caught his breath.

I continued to dust snow from his hat and glasses wondering if he broke any bones but he shouted over his growing giggling, "DUDE?" with tears still on his cheeks, "What's DUDE?!?! That's not my name!!" His words were a little jittery as his laughter became stronger and louder. I never used the word "dude" around him before and even in adult conversations, I never used to word unless making fun of something. I never thought about its definition, so I made something up while I calmed down. We put ourselves together, played in the snow, threw snowballs across the fresh snowy field and maybe built a little snowman. When we were finished and exhausted, he continued chatting and making fun of the way I shouted "Dude"…the whole, long way down the hill.

Later, but still in winter, while at one of the creeks near our home, he squatted near the water trying to position rocks to build a dam. He seemed to have a rather strong constitution against coldness. In the quietness, except for the sound of the flowing water, I began quoting Maclean's closing sentences from his *River* book. I made up most of it at the spur of the moment, but it largely resembled the original wording, telling my son something like, "In the end all things come together into one world, and a river runs through it. The river was cut by the *Great Flood*, and flows over rocks from the basement of time. Trapped in some of those rocks are tiny fossilized raindrops from Earth's primordial past. Under the rocks are words. Our job is to dig them up and use them."

He listened politely, tilted his head with a little confusion but he continued working industriously. Japanese was his stronger language. We never discussed this further. Anyway, he became more interested in a story I made up about *Frosty the Snowman* while we drove home through terrible heavy sleet. It was dangerous. A friend later said, "You guys could have died out there." This is true. I had greatly underestimated the weather.

While concentrating on the road, and trying to distract him, I began telling him how children had built Frosty, how they found the magic hat, put it on his head, played with him, went to school with him, got the traffic cop to stop cars so they could go sledding, and basically, I expanded and embellished every part of the original story that I could remember.

My car was slipping along, sometimes wheels lost traction, and the country road was twisted and hilly. Trees galore – as we cut through the woods for the shortest path home. The entire endeavor was a disaster-waiting-to-happen.

I spoke absentmindedly. Ice quietly pelted and sloshed on the roof, then slid down the windows. Tires slowly crushed the sleet. Our rate of progress prompted me to add new parts to Frosty's story, stretching it out with more and more details, like building up the badness of the bad guy who was trying to catch Frosty, and making the sledding games more exciting.

I gradually exaggerated so much that I accidently made it too dramatic, especially after Frosty got trapped in the greenhouse. I told my son how Frosty was struggling to save the sick little girl, how he liked the smell of the colorful flowers but the warm temperature among the plants made him sick. I described what Frosty was thinking, what the girl was feeling, how Frosty felt when he began melting, how he pounded his big, snowy fists on the greenhouse door, while shouting to get rescued so he could get outside, and how people kept playing in the snow unaware of what was happening, and no one heard his cries or saw him struggling...and then he began to shrink. He shrunk more and more until finally he had become a head on the floor, his shortening arms and hands flailing, and slowly turning into puddles, leaving the magic hat sitting atop the carrot and two wet coals. My son was sitting still and silent in his car seat.

As we pulled into the driveway at home, I was so relieved to be off the road, that I abruptly halted the story. I turned off the engine, jumped out being mindful of the ice, and opened his door to begin unlatching him. In the process, he immediately asked me to continue the story. Frosty had just died as far as he knew. I removed the belt straps, lifted him carefully and carried him up the steps. After we entered, I removed his and my wet clothes, got dry clothes, ate a snack, got some water or juice, sat on the sofa (maybe with the snack), then he asked me again with much concern, "Can you tell me the rest of the story now?"

To be honest, at that moment I was so tired that I had completely forgotten that I had been telling him any kind of story at all. I had been concentrating so much on driving that his request raised only a vague recollection that I had been talking to him, and then more moments ticked by until I slowly recalled that I had been crafting an emotionally complicated, terrifying story.

Anyway, as we sat there and while I tried to regain the momentum of Frosty's life-or-death moments, and also as I struggled to figure out how I would resurrect him for a happy ending, I began to drift to sleep saying random things that had nothing to do with what I was thinking. In a short time, jumbled words came out of my mouth, which embarrassed me. Periodically, I jolted myself awake in mid-sentence and looked at my son thinking, "Did I just mumble a sentence?" He looked at me with similar confusion.

As the adrenaline wore off, and as the forced wakefulness withered, I began babbling more. I fell asleep with him staring disappointed at me. I recently asked him if he recalls any of this but he only had a distant memory of the story in the car. I wish I knew that sooner. I felt guilty all these years for not being able to finish it. He said he remembers it was a nice story.

Integrity is more valuable than, and, in some respects, is the opposite of pride. It's called *humility*.

For the Class of 1985

Chapter 5

The American Revolution and Us

"...One if by Land, Two if by Sea..."

Two hundred and two years before we were born, or
    two hundred-and-one for some,

        The Sons of Liberty had only just begun...
                Protesting taxes under the Liberty Tree.

In 1970, when we were three, was the Boston Massacre anniversary –
    The Redcoats got some first aid and a...kind of pardon.

Then in '73, the Sons of Liberty Partay'ed like Indians with Tea,
    two hundred years before
        we began first grade or, maybe.........kindergarten.

In '74, we learned Minutemen had their muskets ready at the door,
    Starting in Seventeen '74.

And, approaching April 18th in 1975,
    came the poem about Paul Revere's famous night ride...
        which happened in Seventeen '75.

Later that day, going to where the weapons were stored,
    began The Shot Heard Round the World
        on the way to Lexington and Concord.

In 1976, though surprisingly congenial,
    the whole country celebrated our Bicentennial...

We were too young to bake,
    but Alison still won the prize
        for her beautiful patriotic birthday cake.

On July fourth, everyone came outside, where flags were unfurled,
    and you could see plenty a-pretty girl...
        waving sparklers away from the porch,
           and often holding a fiery freedom torch.

-

Even though the Vietnam War was going on, and even though most of my neighbors were hostile to patriotism, I think you and I were raised to be more patriotic than children of today. Orange County was fairly conservative so maybe we were taught more patriotic history than most children in California even in the 1970s. At any rate, the timing of our births put us in a position to observe these patriotic anniversaries. This year, 2025, is our 250th National Birthday with the start of the Revolution.

In kindergarten, I remember we were taught the *Pledge of Allegiance* and the symbolism of our Flag. We sang, "This Land is My Land" and we were shown the map of the country and learned to spell Mississippi. Somewhere in there was a sloppy explanation for "All men are created equal," although we might have been taught that later.

I told my children, "When men made a new government, they wrote *all men are created equal* as a rule to help everyone live peacefully. Kings are not naturally better than other men."

The Old Testament teaches us that no matter how high God lifts one of us to be a leader, we always spiral downwards. This pattern is repeated throughout the Bible. We see it in Eve and Adam, in Sarah and Abraham, in Noah and his son, Moses and the rabble with the golden cow, Bathsheba and David, etc. Mark Twain said that King Solomon was stupid because a wise man knows that one wife is enough. This repetition in storytelling is a way of saying we cannot escape this sinful cycle. In contrast to the Old Testament, the New one teaches us how to live in spite of this downward cycle and while struggling without wealth or kingly offices. Therefore, *all men are created equal* flows naturally from both Testaments.

On the surface, parts of the Bible imply that women are either a lower caste than men or that women are slightly better behaved than men, and therefore do not need specific rules. John Locke, who created the concepts of *Life, Liberty* and *Property* in the 1680s, wrote a lengthy analysis of biblical links that support equality between men & women. I subscribe to his thinking on the topic.

Although it is easy to dismissively conclude that all women must be equal in the eyes of the male 1776'ers, and although I can dig into 350 year old English philosophy to support that point, my quandary with my little daughter was creating a symbolic statement that is concise, age-appropriate and intuitively clear. I don't think I succeeded.

I explained that the Founding Fathers understood the following point: If you gather a lot of men who are, say, only farmers, you will see that some are very smart, some are stupid, some stronger, some violent, others peaceful, some light-hearted, obsessive, etc. Then, if you gathered a lot of kings, you would find the same pattern. This same equivalence is across all groups of men. We could say, "All groups of men are equal," therefore no one is born or bred better than anyone else. For women, too.

I added, "A hundred years ago, modern medicine was very new. Two hundred years ago, there was no modern medicine. Everyone had to do back-breaking work. There were no grocery stores, few roads, no mechanical transportation, or fresh water, or hot water unless you cooked it in a pot, and if someone got sick, they could die in a week.

"Because of these limits, and because men are, on average, naturally stronger, men typically did the harder, physical labor, while women were commonly pregnant. If a woman got an infection, she and her baby almost always died. Also, women had to conserve nutrients because if their diet was poor, babies were born dead. Men are not smarter or better than women, but everyone needs to work together to help each other."

As technology and medicine have improved, people have become freer to do many things that show women and men are generally equivalent, at least in the diversity of their personalities and interests. Women can outdo men giving birth, nursing, and having beautiful hair. But nowadays we can easily see that all groups of people are about equal. Women still have to be careful with their health, though. Where women must contend with a 28-day menstrual cycle, men must contend with a 24-hour semen schedule. When we're younger, it's less than 24 hours. So, though, not identical, these biological realities make men and women equal enough.

Furthermore, while I'm on it, there is no such thing as a "human male species" or a female one. The minimal unit for humanity is one man and one woman who are able to make healthy babies. Actually, the minimal unit of the human species is more like six healthy men and six women because their children will have to inter-marry to make healthy grandchildren. Even six is probably too small to guarantee genetic diversity. However, this rigid demand for genetic diversity defines us.

In the late 1990s, here in Maryland, I accidentally met a woman who had been one of my best friends in college. We stood in a stairwell of a concrete parking building thousands of miles from where we had last met. As we caught up, upon hearing that my fiancé was from Japan, she said, with pointed emphasis, "Good! Mixed race babies are healthier."

She was studying the human genome. I said, "That sounds boring." She said, "It gets under your skin." Anyway, she explained that blonde and blue-eyed people from Scandinavia and other isolated cultures like Ashkenazi Jews and Japanese are genetic dead ends. It's best if people from opposite sides of the planet mated.

At that moment, I didn't plan to become a parent. But at least she gave me a solid understanding of human genetics. She was right, though. My children are healthier than I ever was.

Aside from our genetic realities, another reality of our universe is human rights. These rights are not always aimed at expanding the freedom of individuals in spite of what bleeding-heart liberals say. Tyrants have tremendous individual freedom, which means freedom can be abused. Human rights are supposed to define and secure collective respect so that when circumstances are dire, everyone works together, and when circumstances improve, everyone has looser social restrictions to give breathing space. Breathing space is the middle ground between individual freedom and protecting the liberties of the group.

There is no doubt that 10,000 years ago, cavemen and women, as parents had the same ideas and concerns about their children as we have for our children. We have always wanted them to have good health and sufficient social position. Every shade of religion you can think of teaches the same basic principle: you have value and breathing space when you accept the tenets of the community. Wise men and wise women teach this balance to value individual identity while supporting group cooperation.

Cutting your body to change your sex without a genetic basis seems to be a degenerate act of freedom. To groom children to make them think this is normal is immoral. And when transvestites scream that it is their natural right to groom your children, I only see degenerate hellish evangelists foisting their religion onto the masses. They claim they found the secret to universal happiness but it is all crap.

Advancing human rights must be balanced between the collective management of the group and the need to protect people within many different groups. After group security is set, people need the periodic right to explore and meet others beyond their limited surroundings. This requires a healthy respect for transitioning between rugged individualism and group acceptance. To exist with dignity, therefore, individualism must be taught and encouraged, but everyone must also learn to cooperate within the community.

When Patrick Henry said, "Give me Liberty or give me death," he did not mean he wanted the freedom to wear women's panties. Liberty was a community quality. The right to vote was a liberty. A king sitting across an ocean pulling strings to manage the community was not liberty. Too much freedom for a king enslaves everybody else or it brings conflict as people fight to achieve equity and fairness. Therefore, liberty and individual freedom are slightly different.

At some early age, my class at Danbrook Elementary School was taken to Knott's Berry Farm. Walter Knott, being strongly patriotic, had built a full-scale replica of Philadelphia's Independence Hall on his property. The tour guide told us that he had the builders chip pieces of the bricks to make them look weathered like the real Independence Hall. In spite of this, his Independence Hall was nicer than the real one because nowadays skyscrapers tower over and around Old City Philadelphia making the area feel cramped and dirty. Mr. Knott's Independence Hall is surrounded by a green, grassy park where we had a picnic. I think Mr. Knott had replicas of the Liberty Bell and the Declaration of Independence, too.

Back in the 1970s, much of that part of Knott's Berry Farm (the area near the Buena Park Mall) was open to the public and the Knott family had built a lagoon with a Mississippi River steamboat sailing around it. I don't remember riding the boat but when I was very little, my grandmother and aunt took me there to feed ducks. Once my aunt and I were paddling a canoe and the river boat steered towards us blowing its horn very loudly. That was the 1970s. The Knotts eventually fenced off the entire property because hippies trashed the place.

...

Even though Fort McHenry is here in Maryland and is the center of the battle depicted in our *Star-Spangled Banner*, I do not think the Maryland schools taught patriotism to my children as well as I would have liked.

One day, sitting at our little dining table, I asked my children how they learned the *Pledge of Allegiance*. They both said that they were never taught the words. At all. I said, "You just listened to the morning announcements when they said the *Pledge*?" Yes, that was it. I asked a

70

few questions to better understand the circumstances but neither child had been taught any of the words.

My strange solution was to make a PowerPoint™ presentation. I pasted the text for the *Pledge* on five or six slides, then incrementally crossed-out and replaced phrases with simpler words to help explain the meaning. Then I gave paper copies to each child in a plastic sheet protector. THAT is how my children learned the meaning of the *Pledge*. If Maryland schools are not teaching this then shame on them.

Another time, returning to the topic of freedom, I told my children that English is the only language on Earth where *freedom* and *liberty* have different definitions. During the American Revolution these terms became blurred, I said. I also told them that I was probably wrong. I only speak American and a little Canadian so my command of other languages is weak. And, the debate about how to define *liberty* and *freedom* goes back 400 years, when modern English was new. But in spite of these limitations, and because I am a man, I told my children that I prefer to be right even if it means making people listen to me when I am mistaken.

But: Freedom is the ability to do whatever you want. Liberty, in the simplest form, is the management of fairness. All decent communities aim to maximize freedom for individuals while promoting and preserving liberty for the whole. This means that when any minority garners more and more freedom, they eventually deprive other groups of essential liberties needed to exercise their freedom.

The easiest example of this corrupt progression is in countries that have a royal family. Royalty can use modern American values to justify their hereditary power by claiming minority rights. The purpose of government, they can argue, is to protect their royal right to take away liberties from the majority. Because of the corruptibility of these concepts, therefore, we must always be wary that defending and promoting minority rights can have unfair, tyrannical outcomes.

The above argument is somewhat at the center of Thomas Paine's booklet *Common Sense*, which was published in late 1775 or early 1776. He outlined examples of royal and political corruption then he defined the role of good government, which is supposed to be as small and as focused as possible with only the central responsibility to manage and protect civil rights as derived from our *Natural Rights*. He broadened the attack on royalty to include nobles since they are smaller versions of monarchs.

He was critical of state-run religion, saying it was a tool that insulted God for the benefit of tyrants. Regarding religious beliefs, Paine wrote, "…if everyone is left to judge of its own religion, there is no such thing as a religion that is wrong; but if they are to judge of each other's religion, there is no such thing as a religion that is right." He went on to argue that it is best to, "Mind thine own concerns." This is an important point to our modern politics because...

...In our culture, we tend to draw a line up-and-down and put teams on opposite sides: men v women, rich v poor, liberals v conservatives, black v white, vegans v everyone. According to Paine, these types of divisions mean, "all the world is right or all the world is wrong."

I told my children it is better to draw a line from left-to-right and put good people on top, which means some good people are men or women, some are liberal or conservative, some are even vegans, and each person in some way represents every shade of skin color from around the world. Actually, I said, "Skin color has nothing to do with it," but in our current culture, there is a compulsion to make skin color important.

Common Sense is a long book. People in the Colonies were inspired by its directness, which conveyed simple eye-opening wisdom. Whereas Jefferson and Adams inspired the lawyerly classes, Thomas Paine filled the Continental Army. General Washington required community readings of *Common Sense* to his men during the Revolution years.

At any rate, our country from the 1770s is not recognizable to us. And my historical knowledge of things from that time is based mainly on Benjamin Franklin's autobiography and Thomas Paine's *Common Sense*. I do not know much about the progression of military battles, the economic impact of shipping disruptions or diplomatic efforts to gain allies like France and Spain. I know George Washington became a surveyor as a teenager, and he complained too much in many of his letters. I know less about Jefferson, although in high school, I read his biography by Fawn Brodie. Jefferson owned slaves like Washington but we now know that he had children with one of his slaves, Sally. Jefferson was the youngest of the Founding Fathers; Adams was a lawyerly lawyer; and he and Jefferson died poetically. That's about all I know.

The Revolution worked out well except for addressing women's rights, slavery and establishing fairness across the land outside of the new ruling class. Still, the ideals of the Revolution inspired the victorious Americans. The United States banned royalty and nobility, which remained a strong defining quality until the 1900s when Disney and Hollywood began foisting the romantic side of things. Nowadays, more American women worship British royalty than the entire British population. Most American women also love shoes and spa days too much. I wish we could all agree that it is best to screw royalty but I think most American women want to be princesses. Shame on them.

At any rate, it seems no matter how high God lifts us, we will spiral downwards like when bleeding-heart liberals demand sex change operations for kindergarteners or when arch "conservatives" denigrate the memories of children who were murdered in classrooms. Neither side has a monopoly on degradation.

Chapter 6

The Civil War Era and Us

"It is still best to be honest and truthful; to make the most of what we have; to be happy with simple pleasures; and have courage when things go wrong."

Laura Ingalls Wilder

Because of the distance of time, I am more comfortable remembering trivial things from around the Civil War era of the 1860s instead of things from the 1760s or '70s. Almost exactly 100 years before we were born (1866-67) marks a tipping point between the less-industrial world of our Founding Fathers and our recognizable modern world.

The same is true for places immediately around our high school. In 1866, for example, Irvine Ranch began planting and growing large orchards of Valencia oranges. Anaheim was incorporated in 1870. A short time later, a man named Chapman bought land in Placentia and began industrial-scale orange production using the Irvine/Valencia strain. Chapman became the first mayor of Fullerton in 1887. Two years later, Orange County became wealthy enough to break away from Los Angeles.

Some people will claim that Riverside County is the historic home of the California citrus industry but we didn't go to school in Riverside, so I'm ignoring them in favor of a shorter essay. Anyway, if Riverside County is so important, then Orange County should have been named something like "Riverside County, *West*". Which it isn't. And, since the name "Orange County" pretty much defines itself, the world wonders whether Riverside deserves the title of the citrus capital of California and if, on balance Riverside does, in fact, deserve the title, then maaybee, they should rename themselves something like, "Orange County, *East*"…to set the record straight.

I didn't learn these citrus "facts" while growing up in Anaheim in the 1980s, however. My fractured knowledge came piecemeal over sporadic random internet searches. I think I began by looking into something as bizarre as the modern-day borders of European countries. Spain, for example, was formed in 1492. Then I stumbled onto a sentence that said Columbus sailed to the Americas bringing tens of thousands of lemon seeds. This caught my eye.

Either Columbus was inspired by God to be the Johnny Appleseed of lemon trees or he knew that citrus prevented scurvy. Scurvy was the main cause of death on long sea voyages. However, in spite of Spanish and Portuguese superstitions and their preference to travel with large amounts of citrus fruits (and apparently, seeds), more than 250 years passed before anyone officially determined that citrus prevented and/or cured scurvy, and another 100 years passed before the British navy finally required ships to carry lime juice (in 1860) to reduce death rates.

Following Columbus, other Spanish explorers brought citrus seeds first to Florida, then to parts of South America and later to California beginning almost exactly 500 hundred years ago in the early 1520s. From these trivial points, I recalled reading a biography about William Tecumseh Sherman who became a famous Civil War general in the 1860s. He's the general who did the famous March to the Sea depicted in the movie *Gone with the Wind* which shows the burning of Atlanta.

In reality, before the Civil War, when he had no real career prospects outside of army life, and while stationed in San Francisco to help manage the gold rush following the discoveries at Sutter's Mill, Sherman wrote that orange trees grew "naturally" in California and one could easily find these along country roads. It was during this exact time that the Valencia orange strain was being bred, which, a short time later, immediately after the Civil War, was sold to Irvine Ranch in…1866.

I found an aerial photo of Irvine from the 1960s or 70s, which shows large rolling hills in the background, green grassland midway down and a small neighborhood of new homes in the foreground. Also in the foreground, almost not visible because the photographer was focusing on the wide panorama, was a herd of grazing cattle.

We forget, that in our childhoods in Southern California, we were surrounded by rural countryside and a lot of farm industry. During our years in high school, citrus orchards dotted Anaheim and were spread across vast regions of Irvine and Fullerton. We had strawberry fields and other cultivated land near and around our schools at both Orangeview and Western. Next to Orangeview's tennis courts, when we were very little, we could stand on the asphalt and look out over a dusty field of horses where a few pigs and chickens wandered. Some of those horses used to gather at my home and stick their noses through the broken fence to eat grass. When we were in kindergarten or shortly later, that farm was sold and bulldozed.

Further from our homes, I remember riding through LA, somewhere between La Mirada and Santa Fe Springs, <I think>, seeing cattle "farms", dirty areas where cows were clumsily herded up and pushed onto big trucks. It was so dusty that sunlight was dimmed. When we drove by, I held my breath because of the stench. Sometimes, cow-loaded trucks moved alongside of our car and I wondered if a cowboy was driving. We also had local dairy farms and corner butcher shops.

… …

To stick to the 1867-ish theme, the following pages have brief stories about a number of historical people who did interesting things in and around 1867.

– *1867* –

Laura Ingalls

Laura Ingalls had nothing to do with Orange County or California, but she is interesting because of the TV show *Little House on the Prairie* that we watched growing up, and which was filmed about 50 miles north of our school. Mrs. Wilder was born exactly one hundred years before us, in 1867. Some of you must have the same birth date of February seventh.

She travelled with her family from Wisconsin to Kansas, Minnesota, Iowa and the Dakota Territory because Pa got an itch to move after living in one place too long. When my son was four or five years old, I read *Little House in the Big Woods* to him. I had not read the book ahead of time, though. When I was 8 or 9 years old, I had read *Little House on the Prairie* but not any of her other books.

For the *Big Woods* book, I sat my son next to me on our sofa, let him look at the cover art, then began reading it. In Chapter 1, Laura describes in fairly good detail how Pa hunted deer, prepared the meat and built a "smokehouse" using a hollow tree trunk. After that, she describes how Pa and Uncle Henry (I think) killed Pa's pig that had been wandering around the woods growing fat. They lifted its head and made a deep cut across its throat, then they methodically butchered it.

I tried to keep a steady voice through the carnage but I plowed along. After the men removed the bladder, Pa blew air into it and gave it to his daughters to play with. Nothing is more fun than playing with a large bladder. I didn't define the bladder. My son listened very nicely. He's good natured.

Pa and Uncle Henry prepared pig meat by salting and curing it but deer meat was smoked by hanging chunks of it inside the tree trunk that was capped somehow and a little fire smoldered underneath. Ma and Laura added hickory shavings to the fire over many days and evenings until Pa said it was good enough. Laura especially liked bear meat. Unfortunately, Pa had not shot a bear on that outing.

After reading this story, my son determined that he wanted to make pointy sticks so he could hunt deer and smoke the meat. Pa did not use spears, so the book must have inspired his inner caveman. Anyway, we built a little smoker with cinder blocks in the back yard but we never smoked meat out there. In the process though, and after showing him how air currents affect flames, he got very very good at building campfires with a magnifying glass. Scarily good. Too good.

In another Ingall's story, *The Long Winter*, Laura and Pa had to make "hay sticks" to keep the stove fire burning. Upon hearing this, my son began collecting hay from a learning farm near our home. He'd bring this home, twist the strands together, make a nice "stick", twist it into a "bird's nest" and – bam – Hay sticks make great kindling, which I learned after watching him ignite one. He was barely five years old.

Also, in *The Long Winter*, a point that I liked, which makes it worth pointing out, was a brief story about Almonzo Wilder. As a little boy while living on his family's farm in New York, his father took him to a carnival, where he became fascinated by a man doing the cups and ball magic trick. He asked his father how the trick worked, and his father said he didn't know but, "Never bet your money on another man's game." Laura's future husband learned to work hard and keep his mind right.

The *Little House* stories fall into the same pit as Maclean's *River* book: no one really knows how truth, exaggeration and imagination are woven together. Ingalls wrote well enough to unleash a little meat-seeking, fire-loving caveboy. But her daughter was pretty politically motivated in the 1930s, and she eventually linked her mother's books to a political party. Nonetheless, Laura taught my son that meat and fire go well together.

During our *Little House* book era, my son and I once accidentally stumbled onto a family of deer laying peacefully in a stretch of woods near our home. He took the initiative. Instinctively, he grabbed a large fallen tree branch and slowly dragged it using both hands towards them. When the biggest one saw what was happening, she stood and made eye contact with him.

He paused for a long while. Boy and deer were about two feet apart, gauging each other with steely intensity. None of the other deer stirred. They just laid there like they were tired from last night's party.

From five or six feet away, I whispered, "Are you going to get him?" My son quietly whispered back, "No." I said, "Why not?" He said, "I think he will bump me." Yeah, it was an intimidating moment. The deer was large and towered over the little boy. Her gaze psyched him out.

The mother deer understood that my son was not a threat, and whenever I see her grand- and great grand-babies wandering around the local cemetery, I have nice thoughts about her. In fact, Pa had once confessed to Laura that he had decided not to shoot a mother deer one cold evening because she had a fawn with her. Laura was hungry, and the whole family had gone without meat for a long while, but she told Pa that she was glad he hadn't shot her. Anyhow, the *Little House* books were very influential. I'm glad we avoided conflict in our woods, though.

Canadian and American Borders

Three months after Laura Ingalls was born, in May 1867, Russia sold Alaska to the United States. Six weeks later, on July 01, 1867, Britain formally organized the modern-day borders of Canada. These two events are linked. Russia was bankrupt. Again. In the 1850s, the Monkey King in Moscow had lost a war in Crimea against more sophisticated parts of Europe, including Britain, and by the 1860s, Russia did not want Britain to annex and merge Alaska with Canada.

Americans remained hateful towards Britain because the British had helped destroy the US Merchant Marine during the Civil War a few years earlier. The Merchant Marine was essential for US economic growth. Some Americans, therefore, were happy to buy Alaska. And, after the sale, Russia gained a safer space between their eastern border and Britian's Canadian frontier. As a trivial point, the Alaska gold rush began 30 years later, in the 1890s, around the same time that Chapman was running his orange orchards in Placentia and Fullerton. Oil in Alaska came later, in the 1950s, which was another bummer for Russia. Again.

Mark Twain & Abraham Lincoln – Brief and Random Notes

Sam Clemens, known as Mark Twain, published his first book called the *Jumping Frog of Calaveras County* in 1867. This is interesting because his stories, in general, were topics for movies and TV shows over the next hundred years. Clemens was born on November 30, 1835, a few days after another famous American, Andrew Carnegie, and since I will write more about Carnegie in the next chapter, I wanted to introduce something noteworthy about Twain here. Linking anything about Twain to 1867 though was not easy. His Jumping Frog book is the only thing I could find because his fame began to grow in the 1870s.

Although Twain's stories and manners are linked to the American South, he was only moderately associated with Southern culture. Hannibal Missouri, for example, where he was born and raised, is located at the same latitude as Washington, DC, which is at the same latitude as Sacramento, California. Twain was born and grew up nearer to Chicago than to Arkansas; nearer to Canada than to New Orleans. He was born further north than Abraham Lincoln.

Part of Twain's popularity is not just that he was a good writer, but rather the timing of his stories overlapped with industrialization of the US. And substantial technological improvements occurred in printing and transportation. This helped to spread Twain's books and gave him the opportunity to come face-to-face with huge numbers of people because traveling became much easier. He was one of the first writers to travel extensively. And from this, he eventually garnered world-wide fame.

During the same time, between 1862-1867, mainly during the Lincoln administrations, Congress passed five or six railroad acts that allowed the construction of the trans-Continental railroad, completed in 1869. Britian had destroyed the US Merchant Marine between 1861-65, so building a transportation network over land was supposed to help secure North American territories far to the west and help move coal, iron ore, beef, wheat and other commodities to places of industry where most Americans lived. Railroads offered quick transport with less reliance on water routes. During the Civil War, for example, the US purchased almost all of its steel from Britain even though Britain was actively working to destroy the US economy, and even though we had inexhaustible amounts of coal and iron ore. We still have inexhaustible amounts of both.

One of the interesting events of Lincoln's presidency was the 1862 Homestead Act. Congress passed one of its many land give-aways. For something like $8 or $10, a person, Black, White, woman or man could claim 160 acres of government land with the caveat that they live and work on it for five years. That's pretty amazing. My neighborhood is about 160 acres and has several hundred small homes across it. The idea was that if the railroad was being built on a 20-year plan, then it would be good to plant small communities along the way that could grow alongside the up-and-coming transportation network.

You might think that 160 acres is huge. It is. But if you imagine three families living as neighbors on a grand total of 480 acres, and if these families give birth to a combined total of 12 children, and all of them inter-marry, then each young couple would end up with 80 acres. And if, those six couples have 30 children between them, and these children inter-marry, then (assuming the parents and grandparents die fairly quickly), the 15 new grandchildren couples would inherit about 32 acres each. At this rate, after one hundred years, by 1962, each descendant would have about one acre left. By 1985, you could divide this by 2.5 children per couple, and by 2025, we'd be down to about 0.1 acre each. That'll never happen.

Part of Lincoln's popularity is not just that he was a victorious war President, but rather the remarkable timing of his political victory in the election of 1860. The Republican Party was new. It had only formed in 1854. The Party stood forcefully against the spread of slavery, they were in favor of high tariffs and made the growing railroad system one of the highest national priorities. The Republican Party cobbled together support from various defunct political groups mainly located in the Northern States. Lincoln's 1860 and 1864 victories, along with the successful end to the Civil War in 1865, solidified the very young Republican Party as the leader of American politics for the next 70 years, until 1932.

Substantial improvements in communications allowed Lincoln to use mass media (the telegraph) to communicate with newspapers about his Administration's policies. This was revolutionary. He could almost communicate directly with the electorate, which had never been done before. It was like light-speed travel.

It's clear that Lincoln was multi-tasking throughout his Presidency but he was born nearer the slow talking Southerners than Clemens was. But still, the shared quality between both of these men is that social, technical and political changes allowed their voices to replace the dominant older, stale ones. Twain and Lincoln stepped into their roles at opportune times.

Thomas Jefferson coined the idea of the Pursuit of Happiness, but it is from men like Lincoln and Twain that the American Dream took a stronger hold on Americans. The Land of Opportunity meant that if you worked hard, and are lucky, you can gain three of what Twain called the Five Boons of Life: Fame, Riches and Pleasure. Pursuit of the remaining two, Love and Death, came after wasting time pursuing the first three, according to Twain.

Florence Nightingale

Mark Twain died in 1910, which was coincidentally the same year that Florence Nightingale died. Nightingale was a British woman born in 1820 who championed the need for professional nursing. Her birth, death and major achievements have no direct connection to 1867 but there is a poetic link further down.

In the early 1800s, nurses were generally untrained. After being hired by a hospital, they were treated like servants who were as likely to make tea for the doctors as to do anything useful for patients. In the middle 1850s, Nightingale began writing letters from Turkey where she was working in a military hospital during the Crimean War – the same war that bankrupted Russia and facilitated the sale of Alaska to the United States.

By the mid-1850s, Russia had been a major crude oil exporter for 30 years, which is pretty amazing given that automobiles would not be invented and mass-marketed until the early 1900s. Yet, in the mid-1800s, Russia had begun using its easy money to make nuisances of themselves across Europe and some areas beyond. France, Britain and Turkey did not like this. They asked Russia to behave…Russia refused, so…war.

Although she was born and raised 200 years ago, Nightingale's parents had our modern-day expectations that their daughter should gain a good education and find ways to contribute to society beyond becoming a housewife. Florence became a good writer. She was intelligent and motivated. And, before the Crimean War began, she found her calling to become a nurse, and soon she volunteered to travel to care for the wounded in that war.

This was a major decision that is easy to overlook. Most young people will not give up predictable comforts to face turmoil and hardship to help strangers. Not only did she decide to go to the war but once there, she did not run away. This was her pattern: She never backed down from anything until 1910.

While working in a military hospital in Turkey, Nightingale began sending letters to London newspapers describing the situation for caring for injured. Illness and malnutrition were the main causes of death – not bullets or bombs. She became famous. Some called her an angel.

After the war, British feminists tried to enlist Nightingale to help their agenda but she was not impressed. She criticized the women's rights agenda, in part, by writing, "It does not make a thing good…[if] a woman should have…[done] it. Neither does it make a thing bad…had a man done it…"

As years passed, she continued to write about the importance of having a well-trained nursing staff where women's roles would be unique and distinct from the duties performed by male doctors. This was novel. It was almost a type of Marxism. She defined the need to reorganize the social structure of the hospital by strengthening nursing roles. Nurses had to be efficient, observant, responsive and communicate effectively to improve caregiving. Doctors needed to behave.

In 1859, the same year that the Pennsylvania oil boom began, Nightingale published her book on nursing practices. In the book, she voiced skepticism towards germs and disease on one hand, but on the other hand, she was a strong proponent of good hygiene. She stated that, whether germs had any role in disease was best left to scientists to figure out. In 1867, this began to change.

Joseph Lister, Listerine® and germs

In 1867, again in Britain, a man named Joseph Lister (the namesake for the American mouthwash Listerine®) published his first studies showing that his newly invented antiseptic could be safely applied to catastrophic injuries using tinfoil bandages (he also invented), which did not hinder the healing process but almost miraculously prevented death.

His approach required careful removal of dirt from broken, protruding bones and tissues, followed by antiseptic treatment for many weeks while the body repaired itself. From this and other observations (like using a microscope to view & count germs in skin and wounded tissues), Lister came to believe that the antiseptic acted by killing germs, however, although the observation was believable, the conclusion that germs caused harm remained debated for many years.

In the 1860s, people had long known that germs existed but no one believed that microscopic animals could hurt humans. Sepsis, which is the root of the word "antiseptic", means rotting flesh. Everyone knew that severely injured or broken arms, legs and tissues putrefied – people simply didn't believe that germs could cause the rot. It was just as likely to their minds that severe injuries allowed the soul to leak out and let death slowly enter and spread.

In the 1860s, medical professionals walked around clinics wearing stained clothing to show off blood, sweat, urine, fecal smears, vomit, pus and any other secretion the human body could produce. These were signs of respectability among medical men. If a doctor washed himself, it was an embarrassment. Lister's work, however, convincingly documented that wound cleaning and the use of linin bandages and medical tools soaked with antiseptic saved lives. It took ten years, however, for the general medical establishments to fully adopt Lister's point of view. By the late 1870s, surgeries were regularly conducted wearing face masks, gloves, clean clothing and following procedures to limit germ exposure.

One of my old Army bosses used to say, "The heresy ends after the heretics die," which means, in the case about Lister, old doctors of the 1800s probably never changed their minds about hygiene, germs and disease. Younger doctors had to wait for the old establishment to retire before implementing system-wide changes to make improvements, which explains the 10-year progression between Lister's findings and the widespread adoption of better hygienic care.

Old doctors of the 1800s were like many American homosexual men in the 1980s who were angry about being told to use better hygiene. In the 1970s, SIV mutated into the human virus HIV, and forty years later, we had to deal with Monkeypox in homosexual men. Even after so many decades of hard work, these people still had the nerve to act surprised that good hygiene cannot make up for bad behavior.

Only in America.

Wash your hands and don't put your private parts into monkeys.

Of course, in the 2020s, during the COVID era straight people were angry about being told to use soap…It's the same pattern. The federal government is not responsible for convincing you to wash your crack, your hands, your mouth or any other bodily orifices.

The heresy ends when the heretics die, I guess. I hope.

Chapter 7

My Grandma, Karl Marx and Andrew Carnegie

Before she owned her own printing business, my grandmother worked
for a socialist group. She helped print their newspaper. I'm not sure
how she eventually came to own her own shop, especially during the
Cold War, as a socialist and a woman. Maybe her husband won the
business playing poker. Maybe she won it betting on a boxing match.
But even though she eventually owned her own shop, she always paid
her regional union dues. And, she put the union bug on the bottom of all
of her printing jobs. She was very loyal. At any rate, before she and her
family moved to Orange County, they lived in a small house in one of
the LA suburbs. I believe they lived on Alondra Boulevard, which is one
of the longest roads in LA, but I'm not sure. The only story I know
about that time was regarding a neighbor of theirs. I forget many of the
details, so I am stretching my knowledge.

Don't Mess with Grandma (part 1 of 2)

One evening, my grandmother came home from work thinking about
getting dinner ready for her children, and probably thinking about other
chores that had to be done or checked before going to bed. As she
parked her car and walked towards her house, she noticed much activity
among neighbors chatting in and around the street. After parking, she
listened to some of the gossip, then while digesting the information, she
continued along, eventually checking on her children then speaking to
them about what had happened. After getting a general understanding,

she went to a neighbor's house to speak to a mother who was the center of the attention.

My grandmother learned that this woman had just lost her job. She had been fired standing in her front yard shortly before my grandmother had gotten home.

The woman's boy was sick in bed, and he had been doing poorly for many days. The mother was worried. The company owner, who was also her boss, would not let her take time off of work. The previous day, the woman told the owner that she would probably miss work if her son did not improve. The owner said, "If you don't show up, I'll fire you." The next day her child had not improved, she missed work…so…

Immediately before my grandmother had arrived home that evening, the owner had driven to the neighbor's home, knocked on her door, called her outside, then he stepped nearer the street where he yelled and berated her for missing work. He apparently ranted up and down the street, shouting at the top of his lungs, creating a scene to make sure that everyone knew that he was firing her. The mother stood quietly taking his rage.

My grandmother asked the mother some questions and got a little extra information about the boss, then she told the mother, "After I finish making dinner, I will have one of my daughters bring you and your family some food. Tomorrow, you can stay home. I will see what I can do to get you a job."

And, she did…

When she was nearly 90 years old, I asked her, "What did you do?"

She casually said, "I made some phone calls."

Marxism – What a mess

In the same year that Laura Ingalls was born, 1867, Karl Marx published his book, Das Kapital. Mr. Tozzie taught us about this probably in ninth grade history class, or 10th grade sociology or maybe it was in 11th grade US History.

Marx's economic model has been used by modern economists to define market forces and monitor "consumer mood", "consumer confidence", "consumer production", etc. But Marx failed to achieve his aim. He studied and built his model hoping to convince people that capitalism is monstrous. However, he did such a good job describing economic mechanics, that evil capitalists thought, "This is great stuff!"

The economy is central to our ongoing prosperity, and the capitalists knew a good thing when they saw it. Marx's model helped them manage their businesses to greater effect, which maximized profits. Marx believed that labor and physical effort were more valuable than efforts by business owners to create, fund and manage supplies and all other logistics needed to make a business function. He said workers were always being exploited by business owners.

Instead of finding a negotiated middle approach, Marx simply disliked the wealthy class. He disliked them so intensely that he only wanted to flip the roles: he wanted to make the rich suffer by taking capital from capitalists and give it to workers. This is still exploitive capitalism because he wanted workers to enslave the owners. Whether he understood this or not, he boxed himself in. Capitalists need capital to do their thing. Marx wanted to take capital from the capitalists. He built a hypocritical system.

Workers make commodities, commodities have commercial value, therefore, energy used to make a commodity *is* value. Since workers put energy into making things, their labor is the only value Marx saw. However, he also recognized that commodities can be physical goods *or services*. By acknowledging "services" to be commodities, Marx hit a brick wall. Certain services can be purely ceremonial while others will require intellectual skill, and others no skill at all. Yet, he did not believe services performed by businessmen who used their skills & abilities to conceive a business, or pay for it, set up supplies and distribution chains, and so forth, had value. According to Marx, businessmen had no redeeming value. Had he honestly and fairly accepted that businessmen performed valuable services, then businessmen and owners would be justified for profiting.

At its heart, therefore, Marx was a liar. *He believed capital belonged to those people whom he valued but not to people whom he detested.* Because of this disconnected reasoning, Marx used psycho-babble and thought bubbles to justify theft.

Also, Marx did not consider skilled workers to be above unskilled factory labor. A skilled worker eventually becomes a type of "boss" for holding special knowledge. Therefore, under Marxism, education has mixed value. If someone is highly educated, and has special *value* for helping a company, Marxism compels the educated person to serve unskilled labor. All workers, skilled or unskilled, are righteous.

During the Bolshevik revolution, Vladimir Lenin made the same mistake as Marx. Property owners were killed *en masse* since they represented wealth. Both Monkey Kings, Lenin and Marx, created and foisted their cartoonish world view where factory workers are always right. In reality, the communists were as morally bankrupt as the cruelest and most corrupt businessmen. Lenin plainly wanted workers to be the new tyrants. He wasn't aiming to make a new, equitable society, he purely and openly advocated that the factory workers should be the center of greed & power.

In contrast to the above dysfunction, a capitalist simply takes money for goods & services. This is fair. This is the basis of all businesses since before money was invented. Bartering throughout history prior to the invention of gold coins in Turkey, since about 700-400 BC, was the same as capitalism. Money, in the simplest interpretation, is food that does not rot. It represents work, time, energy that can be accumulated then traded for someone else's work, time or energy. Nowadays, money is used to barter for someone else's work.

If a baker sells bread; that's fair, decent and admirable. But Marx believed the baker unfairly exploited the miller who made the flour and the farmer who grew the wheat. Yet, Lenin believed the farmer was below the factory worker. Lenin's new society made his factory workers the superior, upper class. Yet, under Lenin, everyone in Russia was a slave.

Marx was from a wealthy German family. If he were alive today, he would be the White guy complaining about unfair White privileges. Marx was an elitist who disliked fellow elitists. He wanted to defend and uplift the uneducated "noble" worker who was entitled to wealth either because of their brute, unskilled ability or because Marx believed rich kids were spoiled and arrogant, and therefore, were not entitled to have wealth.

I think that's his weakness. Marx never considered education to be a commodity. If he had, then he would have easily determined that rich people can contribute much "labor" to make discoveries and inventions in the industrial arts & sciences. Those discoveries are types of commodities (goods and services) that have important value that create jobs for the factory workers. Therefore, if Marxism were fair and truthful, then educated workers and owners should be entitled to a substantial portion of the profits. But Marx acted like jobs grew on trees.

Unions tended then (and now) to be hypocritical. If unions dislike working conditions, they should pool their vast resources and out compete the capitalists. They should drive capitalism into the pit of Hell where it belongs if the Unions are so confident that they are in the right, and are capable of running a big business. But I don't think they ever tried.

If union bosses became business owners, workers would eventually see that union bosses are no different from typical capitalists. Marx said that capitalists are perpetually enslaving laborers, creating perpetual class struggle. I agree. But the struggle is always over *capital*. Therefore, Marxism is only a spin-off of capitalism. It is a modern form of Caveman Capitalism. Caveman A did something good, and Caveman B is jealous. Caveman B takes what he wants from A. That's communism. It's theft.

In the United States, instead of out-competing businesses, union bosses of the late 1800s tried to create "businesses within the business". Communist unions controlled the workforce. Business owners had to pay Marxists bosses for cooperation. Marxist bosses told labor when and where to work…

This created an economic triangle: Marxist bosses were pimps; Business owners were clients; Profits were shared by both. Workers remained prostitutes doing what they were told.

Everyone pursued money & power. Everyone was a capitalist.

Don't Mess with Grandma (part 2 of 2)

…She told me that she decided to call a few people to clear her schedule for the next morning. I think she must have called employees at her shop to tell them that she'd be late tomorrow.

The next morning, she went to the business where the neighbor woman had been employed. I forget the type of business but it wasn't a big corporation. It was probably a local or regional store. She entered the building, found the owner's office and asked his secretary to speak to him.

The owner was busy.

All morning.

My grandmother sat and waited.

Finally, he came out of his office and asked how he could help her.

My grandmother says, "Sir, I apologize for taking up some of your time, I know how busy you are. I am a business owner, sir. I understand the difficulties of having to find customers and get jobs done. I know how difficult it is to find good help and maintain reliable, loyal employees. And, I know that many employees take advantage of my good nature. But, you, sir, are a son-of-a-bitch, and had I been home last evening when you fired Mrs. Smith you would not be walking today."

She continued, "How dare you, humiliate a mother in front of her child and in front of her community when she is doing the best she can to take care of her family. So, I am going to tell you what I would like. When I get home from work tonight, I will speak to my neighbors. I want to hear that you returned to that house, you apologized to Mrs Smith, and you apologized to everyone in her family, you will offer her a job and you will pay her for the time missed. Then you will walk up and down our street and knock on every door of every neighbor and you will introduce yourself and apologize for your behavior last night. If I get home tonight

93

and you have not done that, then I will bury this business and I will bury you."

I asked, "Did he do it?"

She said firmly but nicely, "Oh yes."

Then added, "He did it very well."

-

Would you prefer dealing with my grandma or Karl Marx?

Andrew Carnegie

Andrew Carnegie and Mark Twain were born a few days apart in November 1835. In 1867, Carnegie had become so wealthy, that he decided to donate all of his income over $50,000 per year to his charities. In the later 1800s, he became one of the wealthiest men in the world because of his ironworks and steel-making businesses. Although Rockefeller probably out-paced him.

Although Carnegie and Twain were born days apart, and both were members of fairly poor families, Carnegie was born further east. He immigrated to the United States from Scotland.

Like with Lincoln and Twain, as a young man in Pennsylvania, Carnegie benefited from the upheaval from the Civil War. Before and during the war, Carnegie was able to invest in the early Pennsylvania oil boom. After the war, he would eventually build the largest steel making factory in the world. His ironworks partnership was founded in 1867. By 1900, Twain was the most famous entertainer in the world, Carnegie was the wealthiest Captain of Industry, and Marx the most famous (but dead) socialist.

Carnegie brought forth and championed what he called the *Gospel of Wealth*, which said that the same skills and talent needed to organize and run businesses are equally necessary for managing charities. He maintained that wealthy people are obligated to use their business skills to improve society through charitable activities. Carnegie's philosophy was very similar with that of the Roman emperor Marcus Aurelius who wrote that the superior class exists for the benefit of the inferior, and the inferior class exists for the benefit of the superior. Both men, Aurelius and Carnegie, were looking for a balance between the two sides.

Carnegie also championed the importance of industrial arts and sciences, pointing out that America's greatest traits are enthusiasm, practicality, fortitude, and courage, but that education and refinement were critical for continued growth. Compared to Europe, Carnegie wrote, Americans were an inspired, enthusiastic people living in a vibrant, growing country. Europe was withered and dying. Marxism and socialism, in general, were misguided according to Carnegie.

Resourcefulness is a critical American trait that was celebrated by Carnegie but resourcefulness only works when resources are available. Without fuel, for example, your car does not move. If you jam a tree branch into your tank hoping it will burn to make energy, it's not going to help. Therefore, resourcefulness requires refined thinking rather than brute force and simple-mindedness. It requires intelligent planning, understanding and practice.

Carnegie wrote that resourcefulness was similar to *motivation*: industrial sciences used energy to improve productivity. Wealthy people should use profits from improved productivity to improve living standards across *all* of society. Improved social and civic life will create healthier social ties between labor and business. Thus, healthy industriousness should motivate all levels of a community to grow and refine themselves and improve their circumstances. To be resourceful, you must be motivated and clever.

Having access to resources and being motivated to use them works if you are *free* to use them. In the United States, we assume freedom is always present. This is not always true. For example, Imperial China invented many important tools and made a variety of scientific advances that were critical for future improvements across humanity. These inventions and discoveries were made when Europeans were in the stagnant Dark Ages.

Intellectually, the Chinese king had vast resources, which were used by his court to accumulate greater knowledge, all of which surpassed European technology and understanding. However, this knowledge remained in the hands of the king's inner circle. Chinese people across the country were not allowed to use the tremendous knowledge without permission from the Baboon of Beijing.

China had rigid control and rigid social divisions across all levels of Chinese society. This type of organization is efficient in the eyes of racist, South African Boers, and in detached corporate board rooms and from the king's throne, but such over-arching control stifles practical advancement. Without the liberty to use new technology, society does not build or expand. If anything goes wrong, such a stifled system crumbles like a house of cards. The Ottoman Empire of the 1800s and Cuba of the middle 1900s were like this: They each had vast resources but they squandered these with tight government controls and, over time each country withered. They were so rigidly controlled that neither could compensate under economic stress.

In the Middle Ages, international trade on the Silk Road brought Chinese ideas, technology and tools to Europe at a time when Europeans were freer than usual to exploit the new-found inventions and concepts. The intellectual connection between China and Europe, therefore, was essential for advances in things like farming technology, cannon and firearms development and printing presses, among many other inventions that eventually helped to spread European cultures beyond Europe.

In time, however, European cultures returned to a stagnant social order much like China, and for similar reasons. European royalty and noble families constantly dragged everyone into wars and other conflicts that drained natural resources and depleted the male population of the peasant class. The depletion of the land and the communities had a mixed effect on England. Social order evolved. Peasants began to take "family" names as a way of advertising. For example, if Mr. Baker and his family moved into a new community, everyone knew what they did.

However, as social barriers and dynamics changed, scientific and engineering advances slowly grinded on. English nobles, in particular, being on a small island, were always motivated to expand their lands (usually into France) to accommodate their growing families, which put more and more pressure on peasants when a king needed a new army. In time, England entered several hundred years of incremental social contraction, scientific growth and social expansion but not necessarily in parallel or in step with each other.

Carnegie wrote that corruption in Britain lay in noble titles; titles create business monopolies. Titles were social gimmicks that uplifted some families but stifled lower classes in favor of the monarch. The monarch, in turn, wanted nobles to generate wealth for the crown. In principle, therefore, Carnegie was against this corruption whereas Marx and Lenin just wanted to flip roles. This was corrupt in Carnegie's view.

In the 1800s, in Britain, tech advances for farming and mining led to modern industrialization. This brought huge increases in food production, which in turn increased things like steel production, for example. The rise in production & trade (which generated wealth) turned factories into large sweatshops. Improved food production and distribution reduced the price of food, which was good, but this brought rapid population growth, which combined with sweatshop economics, turned communities into overcrowded, poverty-stricken, baby-production centers – without any redeeming community values. It was the same old pattern: economic advances brought simultaneous growth and contraction; greater prosperity for some and greater poverty for lower classes. It was in this environment, that people like Florence Nightingale, Marx, Lister, Twain, Lincoln, Carnegie and others were born, and under these circumstances, each turned their attention to improving the human condition.

Over-crowding diminished freedom & liberties of the working class by increasing competition for jobs. There were too many workers, not enough jobs. However, the working class continued having sex, and since sex and alcohol were the two things they liked very much, they made more and more babies. Overcrowding reduced wages, and caused price inflation because of too much demand for living space, etc. Social mobility ceased to exist because *there is never enough room at the top.*

On the other hand, if your family had established roots prior to industrialization and managed to own land after changes to land ownership laws, then your family thrived throughout these decades. Wealth from successful capitalist ventures was funneled almost entirely into upper-class families, which allowed them to grow and prosper quickly, highlighting Marx's point (or rather George Orwell's) that, "All men are created equal but some are more equal than others."

Carnegie quoted Benjamin Franklin with regards to unequal wealth distribution, "The highest worship of God, is service to Man." Well-managed charities were his key to building social harmony, unfortunately, he ignored over-crowding as the central problem.

My grandmother, too, simply advocated the Golden Rule. Maybe she and Carnegie harbored extra thoughts on population growth, but at least to my grandmother, a growing family was sacrosanct.

For the Class of 1985

Grandma and the Mafia (part 1 of 3)

One time, in her printing shop while she was leaning over her huge light table assembling negatives, my grandmother absentmindedly said, "Erich, whatever you do, make sure you never cross the Jewish Mafia." At the time, I was in high school and never caused trouble. I thought she was getting ready to tell a joke. She paused for a long time, though. Then she looked up from her work and made eye contact with me. She wasn't joking.

I smiled and asked, "Is there something called the Jewish Mafia?"

She looked back down at her work and casually said,

"Heavens yes! Where have you been."

Marxism and Environmentalism – Good Luck

When a population grows so large that resources cannot support it, then squalor and social strain follow. A growing population needs space. Rich or poor families make babies, and these babies need homes, schools, and safe communities. Prosperous families easily obtain living space and consume more stuff as needed. Poorer families struggle.

To manage the lower ranks, politicians need to fracture the lower classes. Theodore Roosevelt described this social fragmentation or "social idealism" as a tool to manipulate the political landscape. Roosevelt's speech on the topic occurred a month after the *Wonderful Wizard of Oz* was published: both talked about influencing and exploiting people.

Dividing social interests among flavors of socialism, for example, or dividing other contentious social issues from the 1890s like feminism or vegetarianism into smaller competing groups, provided entertainment and gossip for the wealthy elite in that era. It was like cock fighting or the competition in the Jumping Frog of Calaveras County.

Upper classes always need resources for their expanding families, which means poorer local families compete with the rich established families and newly arrived poor families compete against the older poor. Everyone among the workers must make do with less. This is the basic field of play. A rich guy who brags about drinking a $10,000 cup of coffee made from the butt of some Indonesian cat-monkey is not a major concern. Resources and space squandered by his spoiled children and grandchildren become the real problems.

Healthy upward social growth requires (1) space, (2) resources, (3) the freedom and motivation to use the resources and (4) a stable legal system with little corruption - to allow communities and businesses to thrive.

Maybe Marx conceived these points but he mainly believed that rich people should be forced to "cooperatively" give more and more money to the working poor. The problem with Marxism is, the uplifted poor will inevitably make more children, which will consume surplus wealth just like the wealthy spoiled children Marx detested. And as a population grows, Marx would need a growing capitalist population to support the growing population among his worker's.

Having only some of the four qualities will not create a healthy society. And no matter how well a community achieves all four points, people will immigrate into prospering communities, which brings more children.

Hence, no matter how charitable a business owner is, no matter how progressive the government is, the economic plight of the working poor will never improve because the growing community always needs more resources.

Even if Marx were a benevolent king and shared wealth among all workers, that prosperity triggers baby production and attracts more immigration, which, in time, breaks the ideal Marxist system. Therefore, communism can work for one generation or two, at most.

Grandma and the Mafia (part 2 of 3)

I said, "But the word 'mafia' is for Italian Catholic criminals." She said, "Erich. The Sicilians will at least give you a chance to pay up. If you mess with the Jewish Mafia, they just send someone to shoot you. Even the Irish will listen to you longer than the Jews will."

I said something like, "Ok. I'll pay attention."

I wish I had asked her why she was so worried about me trying to build a relationship with organized crime at all. I hated my English teachers but I didn't plan any hits on them. She also told me that I shouldn't worry much because crime families usually don't just kill someone. They function like governments. They have treaties and other contracts that they have to manage. But once they go through the checks and balances, she said, then they'll take you out.   I said, "Ok."

Forty Million Idiots?

If California were to build 200,000 small homes for 200,000 homeless people, then California taxpayers must destroy part of the Earth's environment to manufacture, transport and assemble enough lumber, sewer pipe, electrical wiring, water lines, light bulbs, solar panels, heat pumps, etc., to make the houses.

Immediately after giving the homes to the homeless, the former homeless would complain that they need 200,000 new refrigerators. And after they get refrigerators, they would need 3 million pounds of food and 4 million cans of beer per week to live…normally.

And if you give them all of those resources, along with furniture…they will use the new beds to make babies. As babies are born and grow, you will need to build more schools or jam children into existing, crowded classrooms. The community will also need more food, and in the end,

California liberals will have created & empowered a new ever-growing "homeless nobility".

This noble class will need bigger and bigger government programs to keep the "homeless nobles" thriving. And, even if you can overcome all of the above obstacles, and you managed to help all of these people, the "successful" government program would attract more migrants and immigrants from around the world which would put Californians back to square one.

Hence, Marx was incorrect. The government cannot take from the rich to solve poverty among labor because within one generation the poor will make more of themselves. And new poor will travel towards prosperous cities or counties.

The only resource available to help California in such a situation would be crude oil: they would have to pump and export more and more oil to bring in more profits to support the growing population. Yet, in such a scenario, as oil profits are used to support the "homeless nobility", the welfare cycle restarts four paragraphs above where it says;

"And if you give them all of those resources…"

Hence, Marx was still incorrect. You cannot serve both sides. It's dysfunctional to try. Either you destroy a substantial part of the Earth's environment to grow the economy and perpetually help the growing "homeless nobility" or you make laws to protect the environment, stifle the economy a little and leave the homeless outside.

To avoid the above cycle, you must hinder population growth, reign in pollution and economic frothiness (and still leave the homeless outdoors), otherwise, my general scenarios suggest that labor strife, crowding, and environmental destruction will grow because resources will be constantly consumed. Pollution is always produced when resources are transformed into useable things. Life makes waste. It's a Law of Nature.

Capitalism and Environmentalism

Carnegie said that improving the efficiency of manufacturing decreases pollution whether making things like railroads, locomotives, oil rigs, new ships and anything else that could be fashioned by burning coal to make iron and steel. Carnegie's ironworks improved steel quality by standardizing the refinement processes. The scientifically refined & defined process, therefore, conserved coal and helped to make more steel.

His ironworks also made products in any size or shape that a customer requested. This service required improving tool precision and other skills needed to make more sophisticated steel parts. Refining precision and production required non-stop research, development and practice. Research and practice always produce "wastefulness" because industrial education consumes resources. Therefore, education creates pollution. However, improved efficiency from inventions reduces pollution.

Carnegie's approach in our modern times would almost certainly champion using "clean" coal in the United States. Even dirty coal in the US would be ok for making our own things. China's dirty coal pollutes the same atmosphere, doesn't it? *This is why higher education is so important.* American environmentalists might believe that China, indeed, has a different atmosphere than we have…and that American coal is too smokey, but I believe the Earth has one atmosphere, and China's pollution is no better than our own. And, if we use improved technology to promote clean coal, then we leverage our coal asset. We use our unlimited resources responsibly.

Theodore Roosevelt said that ideal social & political promises create perpetual dissatisfaction among the populace. It creates an opportunity for corrupt leaders to foist unhappiness onto average people to maintain loyalty and cohesiveness. This allows politicians to profit from social strife without having to change anything. Complaining is the goal.

In 1859, Carnegie invested in oil wells near Pittsburgh. Oil prospecting began in Pennsylvania around the region near Carnegie's future ironworks. Kerosene had been invented in the mid-1850s (in Nova

Scotia), which made crude oil very valuable. By 1867, Carnegie was making millions of dollars from his investments in Pennsylvania oil. At the end of 1867, he capped his annual income at $50,000, giving the rest to charities.

By the late 1860s, within 10 years of the kerosene invention, and because of the Pennsylvania oil boom which brought huge amounts of crude oil to the US market, whale oil consumption and whale hunting dropped by more than 90%. They say whales did not go extinct in the 1860s because of the 1859 crude oil boom. Fuel was still essential but someone was resourceful enough to invent a new one.

Grandma and the Mafia (part 3 of 3)

Sometime in the 1950s, in Chicago, my grandmother was living in an apartment block that had a lot of organized crime families. Everyone warned her to avoid the wife of one of the lower bosses. The neighbors said this woman was crazy. But my grandmother simply told me, "She was as normal as anyone else. Whenever the heat was on, this woman would act crazy and her husband would send her to Florida. But when things calmed down, she returned. She just didn't like Chicago," my grandmother said. She and this mafia wife regularly sat under a tree in the courtyard and had very nice conversations while the children played nearby. "She seemed perfectly sane to me," my grandmother said.

"And I think her husband appreciated my help."

Maybe this is why no one ever tried very hard to kill James...

At some point, my grandfather's gambling debts became too high. My grandmother loaded everyone into their Oldsmobile and in the dead of the night, they drove away, leaving almost everything behind.

Chapter 8

High School

In the 1960s, my grandmother went to Western High School to meet with a school counselor. My uncle was getting such poor grades that the school wanted to move him into remedial classes. My grandmother was not in favor of this change. She listened to the woman counselor's assessment, then asked her to not transfer my uncle until he finished his next round of tests. The counselor said that she preferred to transfer him sooner rather than later. My grandmother said, "I promise you; I will see to it that his grades improve," followed by some surprisingly colorful statements that she never shared with me.

The counselor was shocked, and stammered something to the effect of, "You don't mean you would hit your son?!"

My grandmother said, "Ma'am, that's none of your business, but his grades will improve. I'll see to it."

Many years later, in her printing shop, I asked, "What happened with his grades?"

She said, "Oh Erich. I motivated him like you wouldn't believe."

-

The summer of 1981 was enjoyable. I was looking forward to high school. The girls I met at Orangeview were pretty and nice. Western had just converted from a three-year to a four-year system, so we were going to be the first ninth graders. And, I felt more comfortable at the high school. The junior high school years had been a chaotic shock.

But soon after high school classes began, and as a few weeks passed, I became very sick. I had no energy. It was abrupt. Initially, I couldn't move well. Then I remained in bed for a day, then multiple days. When I forced myself up, it took super human effort to hobble one slow step at a time. I vaguely remember having a headache and dizziness but the only prominent symptom was unending, dragging fatigue and mental exhaustion.

The pediatrician looked me over and couldn't find anything wrong. After examining me, he said in a deep relaxed voice, "I think you have one of six viruses," and he went on to say that I needed to remain in bed possibly for five or six months. Maybe less. He emphasized that it might be a shorter time but if I pushed myself, the condition could become chronic.

I was 14, laying like a rag doll on the examining table, barely able to speak, barely able to rollover on my own, practically unresponsive but inside my head I realized that if I missed that much school, I would have to repeat ninth grade and miss being around certain girls. It was a dilemma that no one helped me navigate.

Girls made me happy. Some of them were nice to everyone. But a smaller number seemed to be nicer to me than to other boys. One girl specifically had my quiet and deep affection – and in my mind, she was always sweet towards me. I did not want to miss her. At the same time, I had a constant problem with these girls; I never knew how or whether it was correct for a boy to try to tell them approximately the same thing, using about the same set of words while having nuanced feelings towards each. They were each special but I didn't know why.

My vocabulary was never good enough to explain this or, more likely, I never knew these girls well enough to have reasons to be in love with any one of them. A caveman could have probably grunted his feelings just as accurately as I felt, but he could have done it in a rhythmically powerful and pleasing way while standing under the tree that these girls would have had to climb to escape his grasp.

Aside from the nice girls, and the loveliest girl in particular, there were these two guys who, not especially in a weird way, treated me well. Whenever they saw me, they enthusiastically said, "Hey, Stickman! What's up, how's it going!?" Even though I rarely interacted with them, I felt included in their circle as much as any of their close friends. I appreciated that. They were Team A, I was Team B, but they were genuinely cool with me. I could have been in Team A if I had the energy the join.

You may recall that I was extremely skinny. I was morbidly skinny. I am tempted to say that I was malnourished. I wore a jacket...all year...in Southern California. My health probably suffered more than it should have because of this. I was not anorexic but I did not have a decent diet. In the 1970s, for example, my father would boil a head of cabbage and open a can of corned beef. That was dinner. Otherwise, it was Hamburger Helper. Once, in kindergarten, I ate spaghetti at a friend's house, which I said was a fancy meal. My friend was bored and said that they ate it every Thursday. Every Thursday! I went home and asked my mom if we could have spaghetti every Thursday like at John's house. She seemed annoyed. It didn't look hard to make spaghetti but maybe it was more work than ground beef and liverwurst.

I regularly had dark circles under my eyes, a runny nose and lung problems. My asthma attacks were unique, though. They only happened around 2 AM when my father's cigarette smoke died down, I guess. I slept very little, struggled with various medicines, always had low-grade or severe bronchitis, commonly with a raspy cough, and consequently, I was always exhausted. And because of these issues, a small number of you regularly called me "Deadman" instead of the kinder "Stickman".

Many of you, like my parents, believed that I was supposed to be tough and outgrow whatever was holding me back. I developed a bad attitude about this probably because I couldn't keep up. Decades later, one of my aunts said of this, "If someone has a broken leg, do you make them run a race to heal faster?"

I'm sure many of you went through worse than I did. Nevertheless, I wanted to thank some of you because when I began the long six months of bed rest, and had no hope of completing the school year, some of you went to my teachers and collected homework for me. Then one of you brought it to my home, and perhaps someone else came back to my home to take the homework to school the next day. Then you all reversed the process to turn it in. No one told me who did these things. I have no idea how many of you helped. But when I was telling my children parts of this story, I felt badly that I never tried to thank any of you.

Somewhat humorously, after listening to this story, my son politely asked, "What kind of grades did you finally get?" I said, "I guess I got As and Bs." He mulled this over then said, "That's surprising."

His 13-year-old sister, who is a little more cerebral like me, looked upwards in careful, deep thought, as her gears slowly turned. After a moment, she pleasantly said, "Maaybee, your friends felt sorrry for you, and before they turned in yourrr homewooork…," she looked at me and quickly said, "…they fixed your mistakes to help you get better grades." Her eyes sparkled, she sat up, shifted her shoulders and smiled as if she had unraveled a mystery of the universe.

So, whether you fixed my mistakes or simply went through the effort to pick up and deliver my work, thank you. It was nice of you, and it was rude of me not to say this 44 years ago.

I did not miss six months of school. It was about six weeks. But when I returned, I was not recovered and it would take about two years before I felt better, and warmer. I think I was mainly malnourished. In my later years, when I began eating more, I was suddenly warm year-round.

From these circumstances, most of you, especially the happy ones, can see that I was about two years behind you. You had extra time to grow and mature when I was dragging slowly behind trying to stay awake. But because of your kindness when I was so sick, you helped me graduate in 1985.

Chapter 9

History and some Wisdom – More Children's Stories

Imagine a fictional story where an ancient Greek Team A from City A always beat Team B from City B. In fact, Teams A and B competed every year for 199 years. Generation after generation; B always lost. Early in the annual event, after only a few wins, as the traditional victory became apparent, someone concluded that people in City A must be stronger than those in City B even though the Bs were obviously strong and healthy. Years later, each victory proved that God whispered more loudly into A ears than into B ones. Then they decided everyone in City A worshipped God more approvingly. Then their hair style was more beautiful than the B's. The A women and A children were more angelic, the A men smarter. Then, as the 200th game approached, a little boy from City A overheard the B coach tell his team something very important...

The Sneetches

In 1960, Dr. Suess published a story about Sneetches. In the story, two groups of people live in perpetual conflict. Sneetches with stars were better than Sneetches without stars. A cartoon businessman named, Sylvester McMonkey McBean, begins selling tickets for a machine that puts a star onto the belly of Sneetches. A short time later, he sells tickets for another machine that removes the star if a Sneetch wanted to reverse the process. He advertises and promotes the benefits of each machine.

Bare-bellied Sneetches lined up to buy a star tattoo. As each Sneetch emerged from the stamping machine, they instantly improved their self-esteem. They were now just as beautiful as and just as equal to Sneetches who were naturally-born with belly stars. In spite of the cosmetic change, however, social harmony did not improve because Team A was not accepting of Team B.

In a literary sense, the Sneetch *star* is a "MacGuffin". Hollywood's Alfred Hitchcock said a MacGuffin is a thing in the story that distracts the audience, like the Emerald City; once you get there, the story doesn't end and the characters do not gain anything. It's something the characters can discuss or obsess about. After the bare-bellied Sneetches got the star, their social position did not improve and their plight did not change.

A MacGuffin is commonly a magical object that the characters and audience desire. It makes the pursuit entertaining. Indiana Jones only chased MacGuffins. Tarzan needed a reason to swing on a vine. Motion is entertainment. But motion needs an excuse. The audience wants to know why the character needs to expend energy. It's a minor but important justification to help us enjoy the story.

Holding the MacGuffin is not always necessary. The Emerald City and magic slippers are MacGuffins that become less important as the story progresses and as Dorothy goes home. She did not need the city or the wizard, she just needed to sincerely wish to go home. Her obsession about this and exerting much energy to achieve it created the drama. In the end, her basic goal did not require much effort.

You're nice. You are kind. Part of your happiness is to see the hero have a happy ending, like reaching and achieving that pesky MacGuffin. Eliot and his friends helped *E.T.* phone home, but we weren't sure if the message was received. The heroes, therefore, had to help *E.T.* escape...that assistance and the chase were part of the MacGuffin. The aliens didn't simply beam *E.T.* up. The chase gave us something to watch. Had *E.T.* been arrested and stored in a box next to the lost Ark of the Covenant in a warehouse, you probably would not buy another Spielberg ticket. The MacGuffin allowed the characters to be dramatic, which made you happy. The characters deserved a happy ending after all of that effort.

Hollywood stories rarely vary from this pattern. Once you have a hero, the conflict is usually the same. It is a giblet blend of MacGuffin nonsense laid out on a dinner plate. The better the presentation, the higher the profit. The ingredients are the same for each meal, though. What the characters *do and say* as they *pursue* the MacGuffin is the meat of the story. The MacGuffin justifies whatever was done and said.

The *star* for the Sneetches, therefore, was a currency, like a gold coin or like an award at the end of the rainbow. It defined elite Sneetches, and it gave membership to their preferred team. As it became easier to get the star, however, and as the new *Tattooed Stars* (Team B) tried using their "counterfeit" stars to join the natural *Star* group (Team A), Team A ignored and resented the new ones. Counterfeiting works only if high-status characters accept it. In the Sneetch story, the high-status ones rejected it.

To pick on women for a moment, the *star* could be replaced with something physical like the way girls style their hair, or like women who have big-boobs on a Team A, who do not want to be friends with small-boobed women from Team B, or women who are able to strut in high heels, or some other physical ability that can separate people. For a movie plot, Team A has the image of attractiveness, which Team B wants. The MacGuffin gives Team A prestige. Team B wants it – and they will suffer to achieve it, and once achieved, they will have pride…but Team A will usually mock B until the bitter end.

Team B girls, in some regards, might only want to be friendly. But if a B girl gets plastic surgery or somehow changes herself to have the A quality, she will not suddenly be welcomed onto Team A or kicked out of Team B. The movie has to keep its conflict. Whether it's boob size or shoes, the object has nothing to do with membership. The object justifies the acrimony and conflict, which Team A likes. They have the advantage because the story starts with them having the MacGuffin.

112

Desire to be accepted drives Team B. Desire and obstacles create the drama. It's so tiring, I don't know how woman can put up with this. If a movie plot concluded with B girls getting surgeries that help them win a contest, and the B's live happily ever after, would you feel good about that ending?

Of course not. Heroes must earn their happy ending. Kurt Vonegut said that characters must suffer to be entertaining. Getting to the happy ending that is believable requires refining the characters in some way, how they interact with each other or how they see themselves. We want that. We want characters to achieve a calm victory finishing in a safe place where they can rest and live happily ever after.

If characters simply buy the MacGuffin with a pile of cash, that's angering. To salvage such a storyline, Hollywood would typically make the plastic surgery a sinful starting point. The theme would be the effort to get rid of the evil MacGuffin and find a sincere emotional place to stop and *be your true self*. B's must find redemption. B's are the heroes.

In the real world, however, the As and Bs compete on different fields using different rules. The A's always manipulate the Bs the same way a magician performs the cups-and-balls trick. Team A secretly holds many balls. Team B thinks there is only one ball. But B obsesses about how the A's do it. For children this trick can be fun because no one is trying to steal a child's trust. On the other hand, it is immoral to play this with unsuspecting people to steal money.

"Never bet your money on another (wo)man's game."

Golden, Degenerate Rules

For making money, fracturing people among different groups is the best strategy. The businessman, Mr. McMonkey McBean, improved his profits by taking advantage of the Sneetch competition. But, whether the source of division is a star, blond hair, an electric car, a vacation time-share, or some other MacGuffin, the object of desire that divides two groups is essential for profiting. Fashion, feminism, veganism, fascism, abortionism, immigrationism,…Racism is easiest to see…big boob-ism (is also easy to see), all of these are exaggerationisms that criticize you for being outside of the desired team and they all tempt you to change yourself to become acceptable. Transvestitism might project themselves as being an alternative to this, but making yourself acceptable by cutting your body is exactly the goal of the trans agenda and is perfectly in-line with all the other -isms.

Transvestites and White Supremacists are the same in this regard. Both groups are upset that the world around them is not the way they want it to be. They are not necessarily angry about this but they both essentially stand on a beach complaining that the ocean has too much water, or it is too salty or they don't think the breeze should blow like this or that. They are like bleeding heart liberals who are only happy if they have something to complain about…then they claim that if everyone thinks like them that the world's problems will go away. All -isms are MacGuffins like this.

Social competition is never a fair competition between Team A and Team B. There is always an opening for a McBean who will step between the competing sides to profit from their insecurities.

The lure to get you to join a team rewrites the Golden Rule to mean, "Do unto others for a profit." This is the *Degenerate Rule*. Businessmen make the gold by taking advantage of your simplicity and isolation. It does not mean that the members of each -ism group are uniformly stupid, but the money-making strategies are the same. Every modern-day profit scheme is a variation of the Bernays "Torches of Freedom" strategy in the 1920s to get feminists to buy cigarettes. Once you buy it, you would be ashamed to say you can't stomach it. You'd rather be hooked and claim you are proud of that rather than swallowing your pride and going back to where you started. Mark Twain used this theme in *Huckleberry Finn* when he made fun of men from Arkansas after Huck and the Duke swindled them.

We have had "help the homeless-ism", "Bathroom rights for transvestite kindergartners-isms", "White Privilege-ism", "Black Privilege-ism", "Illegal alien-ism", "conjugal-visits-will-make-prisoners-better-people-ism", "Me too-ism", "Recycle-trash-ism", "WOKE-ism", "pronoun-ism". If we rename these *Baboonism #1, #2,...#69, etc.,* it would simplify headlines and could help me gauge our social progress. However, I am not sure which wave of American feminism we are up to? Fourth wave? 19th, 41st waves...?

Bugs Bunny had an argument with an Australian Aborigine where they shouted, "Unga bunga bunga," at each other until Bugs won. He calmly and contemptuously said, "Unga bunga binga banga binga bonga bungaaah". George Orwell said these arguments were like ducks squawking and quacking at each other. The audience doesn't need to understand the language. The tone and pitch carry the message.

A Duck Rant –

Transvestites have the right to be transvestites but...

In late 2024, following a national election, the liberal-ism camp in the United States had the nerve to act surprised after 70+% of the adults in this country ranged between politely disgusted among the Demoncraps to resentful and indignant among Republicans. I imagine it was because of the ever complaining, and ever-growing sexual degenerate minorities-of-minorities who used their overly healthy lungs to make too much noise.

About 90% of the counties across the United States voted more conservative (anti-decency-phobic) in 2024 than in the 2020 election. For some reason, the liberal Demoncraps have been towing this decency-phobic (sexual degenerate) line for a very long time. I don't see the point but the political Demoncrapic McBeans must think it's profitable.

I might be wildly incorrect, though. Exit polls in 2024 indicated that voters were worried about the economy, not transvestites or other similar hypersexual topics. I doubt that the poll was accurate, however. I believe most people didn't want to be called homo-phobic, trans-phobic or skin-phobic so it was probably easier to say they were worried about the economy instead of, "I'm sick of the pronoun-flipping transvestite bull-nonsense," or something similar. The constant grating from the degenerates creates chronic pain for normal, decent people.

As long as the Demoncraps are busy "Biden" their time until their next opportunity to advance the next round of sexual degenerate-isms, the political and religious middle will probably never budge to the left. Transvestite appreciation day every week at kindergartens across the country will not improve American culture.

Maybe I am exaggerating. Most Americans might not be upset with transvestitism. I probably missed something important by ignoring news.

However, here's my point: transvestitism is complex. It's like anorexia, or at least these two things are probably very similar psychologically. Therefore, it is almost certainly incorrect to teach children that one complicated psychological problem like transvestitism is naturally good and another, like anorexia, which is equally complex, is naturally bad. The only reason to try to teach these confused concepts to children is to degrade them, turn them towards someone's religion claiming that it will save their lost souls and fix major problems on Earth.

Throughout most of the 1900s, White Australians legally kidnapped Black babies from their parents on the belief that a White family will raise Black children to be more productive adults. I cannot help but feel the transvestite agenda in the United States aims to do the same thing: kidnap children from the "normals" and put them onto a path to Trans-Salvation, to force children to cross an emotional bridge to humiliate them if they ever harbor a doubt.

Hit-the-bell…to send James Keller to hell. What am I missing?

Transvestites have the right to be transvestites, but they do not have the liberty to influence somebody's child or a classroom of children, or 10,000 classrooms. Demoncrapic leaders must be uniformly wacked out for leading their rank-and-file down this "idealistic" rat-hole. I cannot see the idealism in it unless they are trying to distract people from a list of social failures. Are they saying that if we simply allowed pronoun flipping, then language will become more equitable and society will become fair? Really?! Isn't that the same as hippies saying sex, drugs and rock-n-roll will fix everything. Hippies were just noisy Orwellian ducks.

One way to dig yourselves out of such a wormy hole, is to take down the McBeans. Each -ism contains dishonest members who take advantage of the good-hearted ones. Marx had written that class struggle is perpetual. The social-ism liars for trans-this or trans-that create slightly new fantasies to perpetuate the same political angst that existed hundreds of years ago. Therefore, to be mature and decent, you must identify the McMonkey McBeans in each of your privileged groups then you must stop their anti-normal behavior.

You and your party do not have the liberty to force other people to adopt the language of your fantasies and force everyone to pretend that they think you are a girl with long hair because you, as a bald fat man, identify as a six-year-old named Angela.

Let me eat my custard in peace, Brucey. Or is it apple pie tonight?

But really…where will it stop?

Wizard of Oz

In May 1900, the *Wonderful Wizard of Oz* was published. In this story, four lost, misunderstood characters cooperate to search for a Wizard who lives in the Emerald City. Dorothy, the Scarecrow, the Tin Woodsman and the Lion represent four different -ism groups who are angry about different things but they work together. Dorothy is upset about being lost. The Scarecrow doesn't like the disrespectful birds. The Tin Woodsman is upset about being impotent, and the Lion is a snowflake. Yet, they manage to form a cohesive, productive team.

They suffer. They endeavor. They endure. But instead of finding a magical king (a MacGuffin) in a magical city (another MacGuffin) who will grant their wishes, they find a small man pretending to be powerful. At the very end of the book, Dorothy is the only person who helps herself. She is the only one who escapes from Oz. And, even after everyone discovers that the wizard is fake, each character continues to demand the rewards that he had promised.

To the Scarecrow, the wizard explained that human babies were born with brains but they were not born with experience. Experience is the basis of wisdom, which the Scarecrow already had, therefore, the wizard said the Scarecrow did not need brains. However, the Scarecrow was unfazed and continued to demand new-and-improved brains. This proves the Scarecrow was fairly stupid.

So, the wizard reluctantly removed the Scarecrow's head, filled it with straw and powder, and added pins-and-needles to the sack, then returned it to the Scarecrow's body. The newly bulging head with the steel pins sticking through the burlap showed everyone that the Scarecrow had many points and that he was very sharp. The Scarecrow was satisfied because someone gave him higher status. This is exactly the same as giving the Scarecrow a star on his belly: The new brains had value only if everyone around him believed it…exactly like transvestite pronouns.

The Tin Woodsman and the Lion followed the same pattern: each received a token from the wizard that improved their self-esteem and gave them imaginary social status. And, in each case, to gain social benefit everyone else had to believe that the Woodsman and Lion had changed. If the Scarecrow, with his new brains had to convince people that he was smart, then every child watching the show would see the shallowness. If the Lion begged everyone to believe he was brave, then everyone in the audience would know that he was neither brave nor courageous. The Tin Woodsman stood to profit with his new-found "heart" which allowed him to love women if he remained confident and appropriately focused. Some things can't be faked.

Theodore Roosevelt: Social Idealism = New Opportunism

Shortly before and soon after *The Wonderful Wizard of Oz* was published, Theodore Roosevelt gave many speeches about idealism, manipulation, honesty, and integrity. In one speech, he said leaders who preach social perfection gain more by failing rather than by successfully succeeding. He focused on two -isms: socialism and anti-slavery, abolitionism. Socialism was about 50 years old but political parties had only given it lip service without taking up the agenda.

Roosevelt said that the country had 20 different socialist groups, each believing that it was superior to the other 19. Socialists had made themselves 20 different minorities-within-a-minority; all designed to fail. The rank and file did not want to fail but none of the socialist leaders wanted to succeed. Three hundred years before we were born, in 1667, Milton wrote, "*[It is] better to reign in Hell than serve in Heaven.*" It is better to rule your small group than to be subservient in a larger one.

Social idealism agendas profit by stirring up passions. Fame and influence are more important than achievement. If a leader successfully changed a law or created a new government program, everyone will easily see that the change does not fix anything. It's better to point the finger at a problem instead of trying to fix it. Success followed by practical failure would break the magic. From the leader's perspective, therefore, it is always better to achieve maximum fame without achieving practical merit.

Roosevelt similarly criticized the abolitionists of the 1860s because they constantly bickered and attacked Abraham Lincoln. Lincoln, they complained, had ended slavery only in the states fighting against the United States. He should have outlawed it within the entire United States, they said.

Before the election of 1864, and with the Civil War still being fought, many Americans had turned against Lincoln; many wanted to get rid of him and elect General McClellan or another peace candidate who would negotiate with the rebels. Lincoln won re-election, possibly because General Sherman had completed his March to the Sea through Georgia, which castrated the Confederacy. Again.

Roosevelt pointed out that had MacClellan or a peace candidate won the 1864 election, slavery would have continued in the new Confederate America. The Emancipation Proclamation would be a museum exhibit for its unimportance. Juneteenth would not exist. The industrial US North would have been cut-off from or charged high tariffs to sail the Mississippi River, which would have stifled the US economy while strengthening the Confederacy. Slavery, therefore, would have continued in perpetuity had the abolitionists successfully replaced Lincoln.

Roosevelt defined Lincoln as the wise statesman, the wise elder, the Commander-in-Chief who did the hard work of balancing many different priorities and improvising political moves according to the realities of the economy, the needs of a growing country and managing the demands of the ongoing war. Slavery was one among many social ills.

Lincoln, like Twain and Roosevelt, too, benefited in his career from war and chaotic change. For Lincoln and Twain, the Civil War was the major uprooting event, but even before the war, the Republican Party had only just formed, and Lincoln was one of its star performers. Had it not been for the newness of the Party, Lincoln may not have risen to the top as quickly as he did. Newness, therefore, is an important ingredient for breaking through social barriers. It can help people from humble beginnings rise up and excel.

Newness comes with war. Newness comes from improved technology. These changes can stimulate social rearrangements. This is why the John Milton quote from 1667 about *"reigning in Hell"* is important. Milton did not go to Hell to interview Satan for that quote. He was putting words into a fictional Satan's mouth based on the political world in England of the 1660s. Heaven is the old, established world where everyone is stuck in a rigid, predictable, stable hierarchy. Hell is the new upstart.

"Reigning in Hell" means the path to success and social prominence is easier when a new religious or political topic pops up, etc. The newness is where you can get in on the ground floor and rise to the top quickly. During the 1600s, England had a huge and growing number of Protestant splinter groups vying for God's attention. The Quakers had just formed, and they had been vilified by the Puritans and Anglicans for decades. In Satan's view, Heaven was stale and stifled. Hell was for the ambitious.

Mark Twain summarized this as: "Heaven for climate. Hell for company."

The abolitionists of the United States in the 1860s, therefore, according to Theodore Roosevelt, had the same social dynamics as in Milton's England of the 1660s. And, had the abolitionists successfully replaced Lincoln, their triumph would have given them a tiny corner in Hell with a bird's eye view to watch a new slave trade grow out of the Confederate States. Therefore, Lincoln's re-election in 1864 and his victory in war a few months later achieved imperfectly the desired elimination of slavery but without help from the complaining abolitionists. From the abolitionist point of view, the Lincoln administration was the stale and stifled Heaven which they did not want to be a part of. It was better to reign in their own Hell.

The abolitionists were, therefore, morally delinquent. The pure idealistic position, Roosevelt said, was a degenerate goal; the men driving the movement failed to lead well, they failed to effect good change, and they failed to advance the Golden Rule, and had these leaders succeeded, their political victory would have been the Devil's bidding from Hell direct.

Roosevelt pointed out that politicians use this "divide-and-conquer" strategy to confuse social groups. When groups are fragmented, they hate each other more than their common enemy. When Team A dislikes the idealistic purity of Team B, each group can be manipulated with a glowing cigarette waving in the dark.

Currently, social ideals like transvestitism are MacGuffins for political theater. These give people opportunities to exaggerate their answers for all of life's lemons. Political machinery for putting stars onto or taking stars off of the bellies to create more transvestites or anti-transvestites ultimately increases profits for the McBeans (plastic surgeons) and it creates captive customers who have no decent path forward, so the trans-perverts plod onward for yet another surgery, another improvement, and for social companionship, they try to recruit new, younger, impressionable people to join the trans-journey. This is called grooming.

The never-ending LGBTQRSpUtZvaUePCdYm hypersexualism groups are splintered among dwindling groups but to survive they must recruit.

Social idealism gives corrupt politicians something to control like five, seven or nine wizards pulling levers to motivate five, seven or nine small groups. The audience gets to be entertained by soiling themselves about unfairness. Team A razzles and dazzles everyone with cups and balls, and maybe everyone vapes these days instead of sucking cigarettes in fancy and cool ways.

Chapter 10

Feminism & Cults

During the French and Indian War in the 1750s, Benjamin Franklin had noted that when men were busy building their fort, everyone got along well; they were cooperative, jovial, and well-mannered. Once the hard work was finished, however, men became irritable. He reasoned that a good leader should make men do busy work to keep them distracted and in good spirits.

Men want to be industrious. They want to feel important.

One day in the 1990s, my second army boss and I were walking along a cinderblock corridor. We worked in a research institute but this was a grand exaggeration. The Army had built this post between two large cities deep in the woods near a quiet river estuary for safety and security. Fluorescent lights flooded the hall. Walls were covered with posters saying things like, "There is no *i* in TEAM!" and other similar slogans to foster cohesiveness. Linoleum tiles were no longer capable of being white even though the cleaning staff polished and waxed the floors more often than weekly. One wondered if the goal was to scrub away brightness. Behind the posters and their slogans was a lot of beige paint, thick in some places, but spread well enough to cover the concrete blocks uniformly.

Civilian employees and Army staff tended to avoid the corridors except when arriving or leaving the institute. Pride was important though. Whenever the commander was scheduled to speak to the CIA, for example, he would mention his destination in one of his daily memos that was probably dictated to a secretary, typed by another, proofed by someone else, approved, signed, photocopied, then placed by yet another secretary into each mailbox. Going to the CIA was supposed to be inspiring.

While introducing me to about a hundred people in an audience at the institute, my boss told them that when I was born in California in 1967, he was finishing college in New York. When I began kindergarten, he had finished getting his Ph.D. When I started junior high school, he had finished working for Nirenberg at NIH and when I began college, he had been working for the Army for a few years. The audience took this in good humor, and they did the math for themselves to estimate our age differences. Then I began my presentation.

After I finished, and after packing up the primitive Powerpoint projector, its stand-alone computer and the two all-important pre-USB cables required for function, and while walking along the whitely lit, beige-painted, cinderblock corridor, going towards his office, he began talking about Bill Clinton.

I did not gossip or talk politics. He did. Gossip and politics were necessities for building teams, and he conveyed the importance of this during these discussions. He once said that you can do a thousand good things for the Army; work late, file correct paperwork, dedicate yourself to every stratum of the mission, organize, produce, serve, sacrifice…but as soon as you, as a civilian, make one mistake, they will forget the past and focus only on the error. Gossip and stigma can follow you for at least three command rotations, which is about six years. I gave the Powerpoint projector to a sergeant who took charge of it midway along our walk.

My boss was critical about the Lewinsky scandal. It was not worthy of national news, he believed. "If the guy needs to get off with a 19-year-old teenaged girl, and if she's game, then, let the man have his fat chicks while he leads the free world," he said calmly as he sauntered along.

He was always soft spoken and thoughtful. He didn't lecture in an offensive way. He didn't gesticulate. He shared his thoughts like a father giving careful organized advice.

On Lewinsky, he continued, "Back in the 60s and 70s, women used to say that money doesn't matter in a relationship. They said love doesn't need a paycheck."

He paused, sipped his coffee, then continued, "This lasted for a few years. After they got jobs and after seeing that they made more money than their boyfriends and husbands, they got upset. You see, they were making it in a man's world, which meant their husbands had to make more money than liberated women." I didn't always agree with his opinions but I never debated the issues. He was always reasonable.

He continued, "These women never stepped back and said that they had made a mistake, though. They just changed their minds about salaries and material luxuries, and probably decided an explanation would hurt their self-esteem. You see, their pride comes first."

We got to his office, he squeezed inside, sat at his desk and began checking his email, which was new at the time, and finished by saying, "Some men, upon receiving their divorce papers were apparently surprised, and said, '*but I thought you loved me for me*'."

We had to be careful with email back then. If you typed a draft, edited it, then sent it, our system tended to blend your original text with the edits. The clean draft on your screen was not necessarily the version you sent. The recipient could get something that looked like you were having a mental breakdown, especially if you threatened them, challenged their sexuality or wrote some other chain of derogatory and profane nouns, verbs and adverbs, which tended to be common in that era but which were not supposed to be captured in writing. I knew sergeants who could use the word *fuck* as a poetic preposition, but that was a skill (or talent) for polite conversation, not for eternal enshrinement within emails.

125

My boss continued: "It was the same way with crying." He said, "In the '60s, women wanted their boyfriends to cry. It would help men get in touch with their emotions which would prevent personal conflicts and wars. World peace would follow."

"And," he went on, "the pattern was something like this: the first time a boyfriend cried in front of his girlfriend she thought this was nice, he was opening up, showing his soft side, he was being sweet and vulnerable..."

My boss' office was so tiny that visitors had difficulty fitting inside. There were times when I sat on a chair wedged between his desk and the door but it was a tight squeeze. It was easier for me to stand in the corridor and lean through the doorway to listen.

"...But after the boyfriend cried a second time, the girlfriend starts thinking, '*This is weird...he already cried once, why is he doing it again...?*', and if they were together during the third crying session, the girlfriend decided this relationship wasn't working...And," he smiled to himself a little sadistically, "some men were surprised when they were dumped after that."

Feminists in the 1970s had hit on the ideal formula: *If men have ever bothered you, join our organization!!* It leads to a never-ending subscription-based bitch-service. *We have operators standing by to serve your needs.* Team A vs Team B. Feminists invented "*Smash Like. Hit subscribe!*" long before the internet existed.

In the 1950s, American feminists mainly wanted three or four basic changes: Equal pay for equal work, professional respect, and social equity so that unmarried adult women could live and work without curfews. One of these 1950s feminists had said something like, "The point of our protests was not to criticize men for being masculine. We wanted men to be men and we wanted to have sex with them, too, which is why we went on dates. You couldn't do that with curfews, chaperones, or if a landlord could cancel your lease for being out late."

In contrast, feminists of the 1970s simply hated men. They hated society. They hated women who were not feminists. A person could do a thousand good things for feminists, but if you did one thing they disliked...they'd forget everything else, and try to kill you...at least euphemistically.

Anyway, after concluding with the sexism portion of his story, he moved on to cults. "Politics today is driven only by cults," he said.

Benjamin Franklin had written about the connection between politics and religion, and about the distinction between religion and *sects* (or cults). This means politics to some extent must be connected to cult behavior. For example, Franklin had reasoned that his Presbyterian upbringing in Boston had instilled into him a strong commitment to hard work, simple food and humble living.

Yet, he did not use his religion to convert others to Presbyterianism. He believed that all religions were equally good because they inspired and promoted moral behavior. Religion helped to guide him through the diverse world, which did not make his religion better than any other. All religions provide boundaries to think about. The moral dilemma that we each face is not defined by a specific religious interpretation but rather how to balance personal loyalty to our desired group and display open honesty and fairness towards people across the community who are not members of our particular religion.

However, Franklin also noted that when preachers worked to divide people and foster unfriendliness, they were using religion to create *sects* which promoted *schisms* in the community. These preachers placed too much emphasis on loyalty alone. These types of people imagined that God spoke to them more loudly than to anyone else, which made their ideas better, made their skin color the best shade, their congregations the most harmonious, and their accomplishments more holy. Franklin's terms of *sects* and *schisms* are, as far as I can tell, identical to the term *cult* today. Healthy religions guide us to participate in a diverse world whereas cults build walls to isolate us. When we are isolated, we are socially desperate.

My boss continued, "Back in the 60s, you'd be walking across the college campus and some guy would approach you. They almost always approached the cute girls first but to win over cute girls they needed to have young guys, too; but they would only take guys who would not upstage the guru. You see, the guru wants the cutest chicks for himself, but to attract these chicks, he has to have loyal, weaker guys. Girls desire a man with authority. When the guru tells the true believers what to do, and the weaker guys do it – pretty girls get, how shall we say…they get wet. They feel it in their nether regions. They like seeing the dishonesty and commitment of the guru towards manipulating people. It's like the girls enjoy standing behind the curtain helping him pull levers to make everyone follow his instructions."

We were supposed to be talking about the next main project, which had many details to cover. I had been working from about 6 AM to about 7 PM, mainly Monday through Friday, for months at this point. Back then I could work those hours without much fatigue. In contrast, to those long hours, the typical government employee at this institute did not buzz in through the front door until 8:58-:59 AM. That was their obligation, and, by God, they had those final steps to the sliding front doors timed to the minute and, I bet, to the second.

Therefore, the halls were dead silent for the first three or more hours of my work day. Noises of people walking to their labs and offices began at 9 AM on the dot. Typically, an hour later, around 10 AM, my boss would meander to my lab, ask me what I was up to, and if I had any downtime, we would drive to buy coffee and a donut.

"So sometimes," he continued, "these cult guys would approach me and ask questions like, *'Do you feel like something is missing from your life?*

Do you ever feel like if you just got a little more information, life would make more sense?'", and he said to me, "Whenever someone talks to you like that, you should say, '*No. My father taught me what I need to know,*' and keep walking. Don't look back."

I thought that was good advice, but I was about 30 years old, and I didn't think the new information was relevant to my circumstances. I didn't quite know his point other than the Lewinsky scandal had set him off. He had a teenaged son, so maybe he was practicing.

He went on, "You see, you and I would never be able to run a cult."

I said, somewhat distractedly, "I guess so."

He politely said, "No," and with more emphasis, "it's true. You and I are too reasonable. These cult guys have to reach into their guts and display absolute belief in their bullshit. They can't get caught pretending to believe it, they must act the part perfectly to show they absolutely believe all of it without the slightest hesitation. If they slip, the magic for the sweet young chicks will be broken.

"The only reason the girls hang around is to watch the performance and take part in it. As long as everyone is being used, the chicks are usually willing and wanting to be used, too. Nobody in these groups wants a normal person to look around and see what's happening. It's like that story, the *Emperor's New Clothes*, where everyone pretends that they love the king's new clothes until a little boy says that the king is actually naked. The chicks who want to be used by the guru never want that boy around. You and I are like that kid. We see the truth…and they know it.

"If you or I are running a cult, and it's cold outside and someone asks whether they should buy more clothes or get wood to build a bigger fire, we would say something like, "*Yeah that sounds good, do both.*" This ruins the magic for the chicks. They want a man who knows what to do ahead of time.

"If the guru says, "*I'll think about that and get back to you*," he is just an ordinary guy. The chick doesn't want that. She wants to hear the guru say he has communed with God, whispered to Nature and they both have told him where to find salvation in everlasting faith and hope. And everyone should hold hands, rub boobs and hug to stay warm…except for the lower guys. They have to collect firewood to show their undying love to the Goddesses of Nature to support the goals of Universal love & friendship."

I didn't disagree with anything he was saying. I probably thought it was humorous because it reminded me of things said in the 1970s like sex, drugs and rock-n-roll will fix everything. I suppose hippies in California got hungry, cold, decided they were tired of being dirty, so they got jobs, began paying rent, took showers, bought cars that didn't breakdown and bragged about how much money they made. Music didn't stop; but the world didn't improve.

My boss finally got to his point: "Politicians are the same way," he said.

"They have their handlers, who carefully mold personas, they write scripts, rehearse their parts, and milk their various mixed loyalties. The important thing to remember," he said calmly, "is that our system is abnormally normal. If we replace everyone with feminists, we wouldn't get a new or better system. We'd get the same system run by different crazy people who are equivalent to the current crazies. We can't fix that. If we try to fix it, we make ourselves crazy, too. At worst, we either become abnormally normal and no longer try to see the problems or we get depressed because we try to fix problems that cannot be fixed. You see, the system," he said, "must fix itself. Our job is to stay above the fray and continue our work to protect the USA."

I probably went to lunch after that and told my girlfriend about the conversation. He was a good mentor. Cheers to proper thinking.

Chapter 11

The Poetry of Politics

Going back to Dr. Suess' Sneetches, skipping to the end as Mr. McBean drove away in his truck filled with cartoon cash, the Sneetches, now poor and unable to buy a star, and doubly too poor to have a star removed, are now stuck in their confused arrangement. Peaceful co-existence was forced upon them.

Some of the original drawings in the book display Sneetches with multiple stars on various parts of their bodies, not just on a belly, apparently because the McBean machines were malfunctioning and spewing out too many stars too quickly. Some Sneetches even had one or more stars on their rump. The implication is that the Sneetches were so confused, fatigued and without money that they ceased segregating themselves which allowed them to emerge from their insanity and enjoy friendlier times.

In the beginning...everyone was unhappily motivated to divide themselves between the *Star* and *no-Star* groups.

After the ending,...although poor but equal, they existed in loving harmony because the *Star* had lost its social value. For a while...

--- ---

And by extension...

--- ---

For the Class of 1985

...Imagine, as a few disgruntled *Star* customers tapped away,
   on smoldering cigarettes balanced
      on the side of a large, communal ashtray;
         rain drifting over *Starry Butt Bay,*
            and night gradually turning to day,
               and as time was squandered at the *Star's* favorite café...

One of the Star-On-The-Butt Cheek Cheekers stood up to say:
   "We have needs that are different from everyone else's,
      so, we should form a butt-cheek group
         with bibliographic sources.
            We should do this without delay
               because, non-*Star*-butt-cheekers sometimes
                  make fun of us, in an unfunnily butt-cheeky way."

Others were not easy to sway,
   and they turned to say,
      "But why, oh, why should you work to divide?"

To which the Butt Cheeker did reply,
   "Because it's the best way for us *Star* Butt Cheeks, that's why."

And so, they, the *Star* Butt-Cheekers became grudgingly united,
   across the far far right to the far far left.
      They clashed with opinions and at times socially collided.
         But, they had little emotional theft.
         And as they pondered and snorted,
            they bonded well in that crowded gluteal cleft...
               And, they grew to cooperate,
                  ...so no one felt slighted...
                     ...or the slightest bereft.

When they began, of course, they were a little impeded,
   But in time they successfully succeeded...
      to collectively fart up a social gloup,
         They called the Starry Butt-Cheek Interest Group.

Satisfied and proud, for the unity that they fostered,
    All went well until the Butt Hole King became a bit hostile.
      He realized to help his agenda from within,
        a new movement had to begin,
          which…was a little…awkward.

But, the Butt Hole King pushed ahead with his point,
    by enticing the Left-Butt-Cheekers to say,
      that they had a cheek that was bent out of joint.

And they started to say, that because of their special needs,
    which were slightly different from United Butt-Cheeker screeds,
      they were going to create,
        the Left-Butt-Cheeker Sub-Interest Troop,
        (All because of the Butt Hole's silent…
            …naughty misdeeds.)

Some on the Left shouted, "Hurray!" and some, "Whorray,"
    but it didn't matter which way they partay'ed,
      because their efforts brought so much Left Cheeky harmon'ay.
      And it is from this that they hoped to
      find a higher social station…
        …to support them when they all shouted,
        "We shall always protect the Left Butt-Cheek Nation!"

The Left will say, "There is no *i*,
  in *why*, *we* or *smell*…
    There's nothing here to buy, see or sell,
      but the Right Butt Cheekers can all go to Hell!"

The Right Butt Cheekers would be unhappy,
  this is true, because they say this type of division,
    misplaces blame, when the real trouble,
      is with musical rap and Left-wing television.

The Main Butt-Cheeker Leader, for Right and Left together,
  might be unhappy, too, with fragmentation
  from the Left Butt-Cheeks' dysfunctional paranoid imagination.
  This requires some thought and careful contemplation.

Does the Main, Big Butt Cheeker realize it's possible…
   that the Butt Hole King is partly responsible?
      Could he have arranged to mislead Left-Butt-Cheeky believers,
         to leave in anger, to
            frustrate Right Butt-Cheeker political Sneakers?

This could help, yes it truly would, but only
   if the main Butt-Cheeker Leader and
      the Butt Hole King could work together,

If splintering is managed with manipulation and care,
   then chaotic division will not happen with surprise in the rear.

You see, spontaneous rebellions with or without justification,
   would threaten the Butt-Cheek Leader's insecure position…
      across the Right and Left Butt-Cheek United Nation.

And though the Main Butt-Cheek Leader risks over-exposure,
      the Butt Hole King could always do well with periodic closure.

Though silly, the passion is real,
   like Team A celebrating with too much pride and glitter,
      from kicking or licking balls much better.
         And from their fair play,
            Team A can say,
               that B is not loved by God because their play,
                  has gone astray
                     compared to that of Glorious Team A.

This fakery is too obese,
   because almost all of these arguments about harmony & peace
      are from people crying because they eat too much honey & grease.
      But the arguments are all the same,
         like saying a star on a butt cheek needs a leader,
            even tho' the left butt cheekers seem to be
            much more needier.

134

For the Class of 1985

And tho' Godly they both be,
the United Butt Cheek Star Union together still believes,
they are all better than someone having no stars
down there to please…
Because without butt cheek tattoos, you see,
there is nothing interesting to smack, slap
or squeeze.

And the Lefties with stars will continue to complain that,
the Righties got theirs with too much ease,
from eating too much White Privilege Vegan Cheese –

And the creature who would promote the nonsense,
that the Lefties proclaim,
is the hateful Left-Butt-Cheeky teacher, their leader,
named Mr. (she) or Miss (he) Butt Cheek McSleeze,
who needs to rest for a while,
as he/she tries to quietly beguile, and wheeze,
"They will need another Presidential pardon
as they invade your child's kindergarten.
But you won't mind this because
you are so intelligent and bright
and you don't have any phobic spite.
You all must certainly disagree,
that transvestites are,"
pleads Miss (he) or Mr. (she) McSleeze
"a horrible, contagious disease."

Chapter 12

Freedom & Liberty, again

"Our father had convinced us this country is not only worth fighting for but it was the hope of the world."

Vincent Speranza, 101ˢᵗ Airborne, WWII Veteran, Teacher

Decent society tries to advance individual *freedom* while striking a balance to preserve everybody's *liberty*. While *freedom* has no rules, and aims to advance the desires of the person, *liberty* is organized to promote fairness within and around a community. Therefore, decent people must sometimes stifle their impulses, and the impulses of those who take too much. Freedom transitions quickly into greed.

This back-and-forth is easiest to see in our day-to-day interactions when we take turns speaking and listening. If you do not allow the other person to speak, then you are the tyrant. On a national scale, this trade-off was most visible during World War II when men and women joined the military (giving up their freedom) to protect the United States (to preserve our liberty).

In your social circles, the combination of freedom and liberty is a measure of loyalty, where you advance the success of the team. However, I think this interpretation is usually partially incorrect. Loyalty is a measure of how you use your freedom to help your team *against* other teams. For my ease of brain power, I see freedom, liberty and loyalty as three related qualities instead of different words for approximately the same thing.

I saw an interview with an old WWII soldier who said that he came from a small town where two young men had killed themselves because they were not fit to join the military in 1942 or '43. He said the sense of duty was so passionately ingrained across communities that pride blurred judgement at times.

Another veteran, Vincent Speranza, said, "My father turned away from the radio…And it was the first time we saw tears in his eyes. He lined up his four sons…I was 16, and he said, *'Boys listen to me…they won't take me because I'm too old but I expect my sons to join the fight…this country must not fail…Nowhere in the entire world can a man come here with nothing and look at us today…"*

The sentiments were genuine. Can you appreciate the sincerity from a parent trying to pass along his beliefs to the next generation by encouraging his sons to kill or to be killed? And, to impart this attitude onto his daughters to shape their view of other men in the community? This is extreme dedication. Modern liberal and conservative parents cannot comprehend this: they will ask, "What was in it for them?" Then each side will try to profit while pretending to sacrifice. I cannot help but feel the louder the patriotic noise, the less patriotic people truly are. Sending your child to contribute to the survival of the country is a huge responsibility and burden.

Speranza spent his first few years living in a neighborhood called Hell's Kitchen. Back then, I suppose, to survive, you had to swing on a pendulum between being a tough individual and a rough team player. This is the tenuous balance between freedom for the person and liberty for everyone you rely on for survival, and it also shows loyalty to the group. In return for security and protection, you help the team.

It's not a clean way of looking at things. Americans almost always discuss freedom and liberty idealistically; our definitions usually need to pass a purity test. But back in the 1930s, with the Irish immigrants always fighting the Italian ones, it's hard to believe either side had a common thread tying them to the same community, and to the same nation, yet,

Speranza said, "The immigrants of this country were the most patriotic…they had seen what it was like in the old country…and they knew this country had to be protected."

The most decorated WWII hero, however, was not an immigrant. He was born and raised in Texas. Audie Murphy had joined the army at 16 or 17 years old to earn money to help his youngest siblings. I don't think he joined to be patriotic. He and his numerous brothers and sisters had been abandoned by their father a few years before and their mother died a short time later. The war was coincidental. His family was desperately poor.

Audie got one of his sisters to lie about his age to help him join the army. After three years at war, and after throwing himself into one pitched battle after another, he rose from Private (no class) to First Lieutenant, and earned every medal and cluster for valor, bravery, courage and commitment that the US Army offered.

After the war, and with much fame, he brought some of his new-found fortune to Texas to help take care of his youngest brothers and sisters. We can call this "loyalty" but other words can describe his actions on battlefields and his force of character to return to his family. His little sister later said, "He was a man of his word all the way." He was about 19 years old when he finished with combat. Consider that.

I have to be careful to not elevate the heroics of war. I told my son that if he were to apply for and get an ROTC scholarship, military service doesn't have constant superficial or idealistic pride and excitement. As with any job, there are unpleasant realities and wastefulness. It's a measure of maturity to accept that. We can make ourselves crazy trying to change the system but if we accept the dysfunction too willingly, then we become just as crazy as the things we dislike. We need to strike a balance.

In the 1990s, a sergeant told me that he had mixed feelings about joining the Army. He said that the service gave him and his wife the opportunity to have and raise their family. They had more by being in the Army than they would have ever had out of it. On the other hand, he felt like he was wasting time because he had so much energy to contribute beyond his official duties. The hurry-up-and-wait, and do-what-you're-told-then-shut-up mindset was crushing; and the weight of it grew each year.

This is the trade-off. In the Service, you have less freedom than someone who is out of it. But you get extra benefits by being on the team instead of off it.

I think overall, civilian jobs have equivalent but different restrictions and unpleasantries. Yet, many or most of the people I worked with who had been in or were still in the Army were extremely critical of their time in the Service. I had estimated that as a civilian contractor, in the '90s, I was paid at least three-times less than the captains who had the same education and were doing about the same work as I was. When they found out that I was considering joining the Army, none of them felt the higher benefits were worth it.

People lined up at my office to talk to me. They chatted with me in the corridors and invited me to their offices; in every single case, each one explained why joining would be a horrible mistake. Afterwards, one of the men told me, "If you ever find yourself about to sign up, give me another chance. I've kept most of my ammo dry."

The common issues that these people disliked were (1) brown nosing the commanders to get through your daily job, (2) BS'ing your meager accomplishments to get promotions, and (3) witnessing tremendous waste of materiel and other resources. They were sincere. They hated their jobs. I was unmoved.

In California, several years before moving to Maryland, I had worked for a pervert professor. Consequently, I had to endure him and some of his "boyfriends", who together spared little opportunity to aggravate me with disgusting stories about their homosexual-"*like*" lifestyles. I'm not sure if any of these *men* would openly claim to be homosexual but they forced me to listen as one or the other explained the sexual relationships between words like "annular" and "anus"; they made me work with chemicals that smelled like rotting, concentrated semen, told stories about bathhouse adventures in San Francisco, anal sex at Black's Beach in San Diego, and defined things like *feltching*. One time, I think at a convention in Anaheim of all places, they invited me to their hotel room to meet before going to breakfast. One of them was still in bed, covered with a sheet while masturbating. I went back to the hall. They remained inside, smug and happy.

At that time, I kept to myself. I regularly worked all week then drove 130 miles to visit my baby niece who was fatherless, and by my measure was stuck in her dysfunctional world. To be a positive influence for her, I spent most of my free time with her instead of interacting with my coworkers. In return, my coworkers seemed to think I must have been living some kind of secret degenerate life, and they thought it was funny to spread gossip and try to figuratively ass fuck me with fake gossip in their spare time.

So, returning to the negative advice about joining the Army…if some LTC or COL is going to expect me to attend church services twice or three times a week in exchange for my next preferred duty station, that's easy. Bring it on. As long as the homosexual bullshit is stifled, I'm good with just about anything.

Alas…my lungs were no good. In high school, around 1984 or '85, recruiters approached me and tried to get me to sign up for the Army. Even the Navy and Marines tried recruiting me. Bad lung function was an instant disqualification. The same was true in the 1990s. I was out before I was ever in.

Still, the military offers magnificent education opportunities for job training that are largely unique from anything that colleges or states can offer. If your enlistment contract includes your career interests, then the Service is obligated to train you in that. And if you do not have the aptitude for your chosen job path, then they will try to find a better fit. I hope it's fair to say that you get out of it what you put in, but I suppose that will vary on circumstances and luck.

In terms of other payouts, they will make your body as physically healthy as you can be, and if you add the health insurance, housing allowance, vacation time, moving costs and other benefits for being in the Service, compared to spending four or five years in college, I preferred that my son and daughter apply for ROTC and put a few years in one of the Armed Services. By serving their country, their country can train them and give them a career that they can use to build a family. The motive can be superficial and self-serving, but that will be decided by the integrity of each person. Do your best.

The dedication of Americans from the 1940s and 1950s is starkly contrasted with our country today where the porn whores and their pimps foist incest films to celebrate their degenerate "happiness", have their noisy influence, show off their cracks at playgrounds, and who have no sense of maturity or loyalty to this country beyond paying their dermatologist, plastic surgeons, orthodontists, hair stylists, and a list of other cock suckers who I have not considered.

These pimps & whores do not consider obligation and grief to be qualities of a good, decent life. Decency requires a balance. Indecency does not, and currently our society encourages these absurd, never ending trans-this, trans-that and trans-fat distractions. When decent people give away the liberties of a community for fear of offending the anti-normals, we give the degenerates too much freedom. They become a degraded nobility. We become their servants. And they will come back for more.

Frederick Douglass wrote that a slave is someone waiting to be set free. If you are like me, then my advice is that we should stop waiting. We do not have to continuously diminish ourselves and our integrity for fear that we will offend bad people. Part of the reason I wrote this book is because I am too damned tired to anticipate the complaints from every walking sack of shit that wants me to shut-up. You and I are not toxic. They are.

Balancing freedom with liberty can be complicated. Government programs will never work because age, health disparities and wealth-gaps create massive social distinctions that can never be well-managed by mechanical bureaucracies. At best, government can protect liberties. For freedom, in practice, each person must be fiercely loyal to concepts in the Declaration of Independence and to the Golden Rule. This behavior, these loyalties cannot be legislated. Everything else is pride and pretense.

Struggle, hardship and grief should not be welcomed into our lives but each of these are parts of a mature life. Anti-decency scum deprive us of the time and ability to manage our social values. They encourage more and more addiction and more razzle & dazzle, they are constantly moving the cups and balls pretending to be smart. They degenerate into tyrants, and as tyrants, they respect only themselves. You and your children are nothing more than crushed, partially burned cigarettes.

Regardless of the era or the place, the more we pamper the idealists, the more selfish and self-absorbed they become. There's a time and a place for all things. These times and places must be defended by good people. We set the standard with the Golden Rule but when our fair treatment and good behavior are not returned by the scum, then it is our duty to reject them. We get to ring the bell and send the degenerates away. And, hopefully, forever. *It is our right and our children's right to be well.* Instead, the evil ones hit us with emotional bombshells. Enough already. It's our right to send these scum back where they belong, back to the hole they crawled out of.

Each community has young children who must grow to be responsible. We hope to surround them with happiness and security so that they can grow and gain experience in age-appropriate ways through each stage of childhood. As children of the 1970s and 80s, we were probably left to our own devices at relatively young ages. My moral compass was set by my grandmother, but I was tossed into the fray pretty quickly.

Theodore Roosevelt wrote, "The boy can best become a good man by being a good boy…". A good boy was fearless, stalwart, hated and feared by all that is wicked and depraved, incapable of submitting to wrong-doing. The modern equivalent for girls is the same. Good boys and girls are supposed to be "tender to the weak and helpless," and "capable of giving a bad boy a thrashing, as the need arises."

But, in crowded metropolitan cities or on faceless internet chat platforms, goodness is compromised. Children are easily led astray and are always surrounded by degenerates. We cannot protect children as lone parents managing all the aspects of a home life. Like with soldiers fighting tyrants, one or two parents need the help of a well-organized army. Yet, bureaucracies cannot help much beyond semi-corrupt or inept school boards or extended family relations who have their own delinquencies and dubious characters.

The world is dirty. We have to deal with that. Our purpose as adults is to teach. We teach in our manners and actions with everything we do even when sleeping on sofas or watching TVs. We are supposed to defend the borders of schools so that children can have fun and games, and so they can learn social skills, distinguish good from bad, decent vs indecent, necessary and unnecessary, etc. This helps them balance desire.

We can teach our children a small number of life skills and try to impart wisdom while playing along creeks and streams, or walking through the woods, but these lessons are probably too few and, in some ways, too detached from hustling on the internet. We, as parents and adults, are the innumerable one-man and one-woman armies. We are the Audie Murphy-ies and Speranzas. We exist to defend and teach our children, whether in our homes, communities, and across our states, and for the benefit of our country. But ultimately, the goal of such education is to set our children free. They are entitled to have complete liberty provided they have good morals and behave decently. Indecent scum who take advantage of our good natures must be punished.

The only thing easy about being a parent is screwing up. Do we believe that this country is worth defending and that it is supposed to be the hope of the world? If we can properly define our national priorities, and filter the noise from fractured interest groups, then we can defend our communities well. Being fair and honest is easy compared to fighting against degenerates.

Returning briefly to the real and accurate Maclean quote: "*In the end all things merge into one and a river runs through it. It was cut from the world's great flood and flows over rocks from the basement of time. On some of the rocks are timeless raindrops. Under the rocks are words and some of the words are theirs.*" I wonder…beyond 2025, will you use these words well? Or will we continue to stand on opposite sides of a chasm; the right side having to always face down the anti-decent left?

Let me transition to transvestites one final time: As far as I can tell, the modern-day trans-crusade began by aiming to "free" transvestite kindergarteners. This is strong evidence that transvestites were targeting not just bleeding-heart adults but little children, too. Who targets little children in political fights? In fact, the transvestite social strategy was focused not just on children but it aimed with laser beam precision straight between their legs. "Toilet rights" were dangled and banged around as if Adolf Hitler had returned from the dead. And, transvestites were here to defend the rim.

We like to think that psychology is a medical science intended to help improve people. Bernays, who in the 1920s convinced feminists to smoke cigarettes to show their strength, was the nephew of Sigmund Freud. Freud is the father of psychoanalysis. Freud, in turn, was a sexual degenerate who foisted his anal obsessions onto the world by teaching everyone that if children are not allowed to pick their butts and have sexual fantasies with their parents, that children will grow up to become homosexual. Freud's daughter, Anna, taught girls up until the early 1980s that all women naturally want to be raped and beaten. The founding principles of psychology set in the earliest years of the 1900s were driven by sexual degeneracy and corporate greed.

In the 1980s, when the medicine Ritalin was being prescribed to children for OCD and ADHD, and the best commercial goal for managing these children was to sedate them with prescription psychotropic drugs; behind-the-scenes, the rule of thumb was that children were screwed up because of insanity in the home. Home life was where the tightly wound emotional problems grew.

After my daughter was born, a nurse told me that my goal should be to raise my children right. I agreed. She clarified: "I mean, when your child turns 18, you want her to be able to pay for her own therapy." After I caught my breath and put my eyes back into my head, I laughed.

The problem, I think, is that over recent decades, children have become more and more aware of psychological manipulation and sexual aggressiveness from degenerates but they do not have adequate power to defend themselves from such horrid people. To make money, you must convince people to buy stuff. As customers become aware of your tricks, you must target more naïve customers. That is how the degenerate hypersexual agenda works. And most parents and schools refuse to stop this manipulation for fear of offending someone.

In the current transvestite era, littlest children are the target audience. If anyone in the trans-community disagrees with this, they are being dishonest. Trans-activists are no different from White supremacists. Both groups are upset that the world is not perfect. Both groups believe that if everyone saw the world correctly, then all the problems of the world would go away. Both groups might as well stand on a beach and complain that the ocean has too much water, or that the breeze should not blow this way or that way. Both groups have the same goals. The trans-agenda is not unique except they have managed to go directly for children, by-passing parents, aiming for the cracks between children's legs.

In the 1980s, another rule-of thumb was that someone who is sexually abused as a child tends to abuse children as adults. They repeat & perpetuate the pattern. If it is known that adult transvestites are child abuse victims, then based on their toilet agenda, I believe transvestites are trying to repeat & perpetuate this abuse to extend their sexual fantasies deeper into the real world beyond the simple Goth world of freedom for the individual. They want to force us to swallow everything they ram down our children's throats.

Similarly, they aim to achieve the same political and legal coverage that feminists have gained – the freedom to be deviant in the classroom; to repeat & perpetuate with no liabilities, and to satisfy their desire to pursue their happiness with someone else's child. Once courts institutionalize these patterns of behavior, judges follow along like mules.

The anti-normals do not want parents to have meaningful leverage to speak out against the main thrust of the collective degenerate sexual agenda; they want the freedom to subjugate children at any school by using trans-sympathetic teachers and trans-sympathetic principals to foist degenerate stories to "molest" children as young as they can reach. The devil aims to corrupt the youngest first.

At present, these decency-phobic groups do not have the liberty to influence your children or grandchildren in most schools but this insulation is diminishing. They are Biden their time for the next best opportunity. Therefore, granting such freedom to transvestite operatives enslaves rather than improves good people. Since the world is dirty and not an ideal place, it remains our collective right to put down the transvestite agenda and stop it in its tracks, forever.

My old Army boss used to say, "Never bullshit a bullshitter."

We are so fractured among different selfish tribes that it's usually too difficult to tell which rat stinks the most. The transvestite agenda seems to make it easier to sniff out the trouble…although, maybe it's just me,

Mr. James Erich Keller,
Candidate: King of the Assholes, USA.
Platform: Anti-decency-phobes all the way.
Personal: Does not own an EV but has a vision.
Identifies as: A man…who does not watch TV
(aka - television).

For the Class of 1985

Afterward

Benjamin Franklin reasoned that God must value American concepts of Natural Law, Free Will and Reason encompassed in the peaceful aims of the 1770s during negotiations with Britain. He further believed that God must have favored the colonies as they went to war to defend these principles of liberty against the most powerful country in the world. The fathers of this country were flawed - Perfection is not a human quality. Yet, God's Grace, Franklin believed, was given as a reward to those Patriots who championed these new American ideals through their hard thinking and hard work to form the sound foundation of this new country. This is what "...one Nation under God..." means, as I told my children. God's Grace is the foundation and a protective cover. We build our integrity on that foundation and try to protect it from those who want to debase it, and push it off the stable, sacred ground. But, the world wonders, and I wonder, too, whether the lyrics, "..God shed his Grace on thee..." refer to a lost, distant past, and that God has finished with us, and He has moved on, ignoring our degenerate need for constant distraction, or are the lyrics a constant request, a prayer, for His wisdom to guide the present and future of this country; to help us escape the devil's grip, and give us the strength to slap the devil away when it comes back to enslave us again.

--- ---

My grandmother knew the world was not perfect. But she navigated the competition between reality and idealism. She was in favor of practicality and decency. She felt fairness should be rewarded and that we should follow the Golden Rule. The last time I saw her she said, "Erich, I used to believe that if people had the chance, they would always make the correct decisions to be fair and considerate to their fellow man. I'm not so sure now." She was in her 90's. That is what the machinations from the "news" and Google machines have achieved. That is what they have snuffed out – the right for normal people to exist with dignity.

www.ingramcontent.com/pod-product-compliance
Lightning Source LLC
Chambersburg PA
CBHW071858020426
42331CB00010B/2563